March 20, 2011

To: Susan

In Christ -

In Love,

Klatha Lee
Brown

TO GOD BE THE GLORY

daily

devotions

that will help

the reader

recognize God's Voice

by

Hatha Lee Brown

2005 Preston Rd.
Eau Claire WI, 54703

Foreword

A primary purpose of this daily devotional is to encourage the reader to get acquainted with scriptures and recognize God's plan for his/her life.

There are more than 200 indexed Bible references in this book. If used daily, it will encourage the reader and give soul refreshment needed for these challenging times in which we live.

My prayer is for each person to see the uncom-promising truths of scripture and experience them by the power of the Holy Spirit. God can then use these pages to give more of Himself to those who ask.

To God be the Glory.

Donna L. Mitchell, Editor

Acknowledgements

--- **Grace Knafel** has written and composed many beautiful songs that glorify God. We are blessed to have her permission to print the words to some of her songs in this book. You can listen to Gracie's songs at→ www.gracesongs.net.

--- **Jackie Wakeman** did the graphic design, and she was able to capture the essence of God's glory on the book's cover.

--- I am so grateful to my husband, **Terry Brown**, for his love and encouragement during the long writing process.

--- <u>To God Be The Glory</u> would only be a dream if it had not been for my friend, **Donna Mitchell,** who encouraged me to continue writing this book. Her friendship has been one of the greatest blessings that God has ever given to me. Many times, she would remind me that when God asks us to do something for Him, He also gives us the ability to do it. I wish I could adequately express my appreciation for the many hours she spent editing this book. Donna's expertise has truly been a godsend. Thank you, my dear friend.

--- I dedicate this book to my Lord and Savior, **Jesus Christ**. I truly know that I was only a vehicle for the Holy Spirit who wrote His book through me. I give Him all the glory for calling me into action for such a time as this.

Preface

I know and believe with all my heart that Jesus Christ is the only way to God the Father. My life changed forever when I accepted Jesus Christ as my personal Savior. Before my surrender to Christ, I struggled through life with failed relationships, the death of a daughter, the death of a spouse, the death of a sister and many other struggles.

As you make daily references to <u>To God Be The Glory</u>, I pray that the Scriptures will speak to you and expand your vision of what God can do in your life. Accepting Christ and surrendering your life to Him are the most important decisions you will ever make. Your life too will be changed forever.

I am also praying that you will be challenged and better equipped to recognize the glory of God that is everywhere.

Hatha Lee Brown

"Ask, and it will be given to you; seek, and you will find; knock, and it will be opened to you."
Matthew 7:7 NASB

~~ This scripture gives us directions for seeking God. This verse does not say that it might be given to us, but that it will be given. Why do we wrestle with earthly problems instead of giving it to the One who can help us in any situation?

God is waiting. He has made the directions very clear. Ask, seek and knock. God always keeps His promises when we seek Him. ~~

Thought for the Day

Lift the scales from your eyes and let total faith prevail.

To God Be The Glory

Praise the LORD, for the LORD is good; sing praise to His name, for that is pleasant. *Psalm 135:3 NIV*

~~ In this verse and throughout the Psalms there is a consistent pattern that the Lord is good. The Lord has given us life and everything we need to live our lives. In addition to an earthly life, we have been given eternal life. The Lord is everything to the true believer. Let us praise the LORD and sing praises to His name. Let us bow down and worship our LORD, for the LORD is good now and forever. ~~

Thought for the Day

Sing praises to the LORD.

In all my prayers for all of you, I always pray with joy because of your partnership in the gospel from the first day until now. *Philippians 1:4-5 NIV*

~~ The Philippians helped Paul spread the Gospel by financially supporting him while he was in prison. We too can help spread the Gospel of Jesus Christ by helping our ministers, missionaries and evangelists. Our gifts and prayers can help millions learn about Jesus Christ and His gift of eternal life with Him. ~~

Thought for the Day

Help lead souls to Christ.

God called to him from within the bush, "Moses! Moses!" And Moses said, "Here I am." *Exodus 3:4b NIV*

~~ Moses was drawn to the burning bush. It was burning, but not being consumed by the fire. From the burning bush God called out to Moses and he answered Him, "Here I am." When God calls our names we must be ready to tell Him, "Here I am." ~~

Thought for the Day

Be ready always to hear God.

Brethren, I do not count myself to have appre-
hended; but one thing I do, forgetting those things
which are behind and reaching forward to those
things which are ahead. *Philippians 3:13 NKJV*

~~ When we ask God for forgiveness, He forgives us and it
is forgotten.

There are also devoted believers who will take us under their
wings and God will use them to show us that He loves us
dearly. Through this encouragement we will see that God
has a purpose for our lives. As we talk to the Lord, He will
reveal what He has planned for us. He gives us talents and
we are to use those talents for His glory. Don't look back
but look forward to serving God and to eternal life. ~~

Thought for the Day

Seek the Lord with all your heart and soul.

A time to be silent and a time to speak.
Ecclesiastes 3:7b NASB

~~ Many times I have heard the statement, "If you do not have something good to say, don't say anything." That sounds like sound judgment; and the scripture also tells us there is a time to speak.

When we feel we are compelled to speak, let us ask God to inject the words into our mouths that fulfill His will, not ours. ~~

Thought for the Day

Lord, help us to reflect Your goodness and love to others.

Do not be overcome by evil, but overcome evil with good. *Romans 12:21 NASB*

~~ There are times when we are striving to serve God that the enemy will attack us. The attack is meant to divert our attention away from God. When we are away from God we do not have the armor to fight evil.

Evil is a destroyer. We are to cling close to the Lord and return evil with forgiveness and goodness. This is only possible when we have a God-filled life. ~~

Thought for the Day

The Lord will vindicate His children.

The unfolding of Your words gives light; it gives understanding to the simple. *Psalm 119:130 NIV*

~~ The Bible is our "road map" for our lives. The Word gives us "the light" needed for our journey with God. Without the light we would be walking in the darkness, unable to see the pathway God has opened for us to follow.

Seek God by reading and studying the Bible. He will flood your life with overflowing peace, joy and light. His Word will give you understanding that you never thought possible. ~~

Thought for the Day

Be a follower of God's light.

We love, because He first loved us. *1 John 4:19 NIV*

~~ God allowed His only Son to die a terrible death on the cross for you and me. He conquered death for our salvation.

Love of the flesh can be lost for no reason. The love God has for us is "forever love". His love is absolute; it does not change. We can return God's love by keeping His commandments. ~~

Thought for the Day

God's love is forever true.

A friend loves at all times. *Proverbs 17:17a NIV*

~~ We are richly blessed when we have a friend that is loyal at all times. We are even more blessed when our friend is in Christ. Christ connects us together with heart, soul and mind. Dear friends are there to help each other on their journey to Christ. ~~

Thought for the Day

Be a friend that loves at all times.

A gossip betrays a confidence, but a trustworthy man keeps a secret. *Proverbs 11:13 NIV*

~~ The book of Proverbs provides instruction to live by that enriches our lives and the lives of others.

We need to remember that when we gossip we betray others, ourselves, but most of all, we grieve our Lord. We become the losers. ~~

Thought for the Day

Let your words be uplifting.

For we must all appear before the judgment seat of Christ, so that each one may be recompensed for his deeds in the body, according to what he has done, whether good or bad. *2 Corinthians 5:10 NASB*

~~ Are you prepared to meet Christ at judgment time? Have your deeds been to glorify God?

All Christians will kneel before Christ. He will know what we have done and what we have left undone. While we are here on earth we can hide things or pretend; but Christ will know the truth when we stand before Him.

Will our deeds bring joy and honor to our Father at judgment day? ~~

Thought for the Day

May our works glorify God - not the world.

Yet those who wait for the Lord will gain new strength; they will mount up with wings like eagles, they will run and not get tired, they will walk and not become weary. *Isaiah 40:31 NASB*

~~ The word "wait" means "to hope," to look to God for everything we need. This involves praying to Him, meditating on His character and His promises and seeking to glorify Him in everything we do or say. During our wait, God enables us to soar when there is a crisis, to run when the challenges are many, and to walk with faith in the day-to-day demands of life. ~~

Thought for the Day

Our strength comes from God.

"Come to Me, all you who are weary and heavy-laden, and I will give you rest." *Matthew 11:28 NASB*

~~ Often we have to stop whatever we are doing and ask God to give us the strength to do what is before us.

When we go to Christ we are putting our total trust in Him. He is the only way to lessen our burdens and receive the love and peace that only Christ can give us. Everything on earth is temporary; but Christ will take us through our lives, refreshing our souls all the way.

All we need to do is answer His call to come to Him. ~~

Thought for the Day

Christ will refresh your life with true meaning.

Peace I leave with you; My peace I give to you; not as the world gives do I give to you. Do not let your heart be troubled, nor let it be fearful.
John 14:2 7 NASB

~~ In the world, a person's "peace" is based on personal ability, but the Christian depends on spiritual knowledge in Christ. People in the world depend on externals, but Christians depend on their faith and the eternals.

In God's Word, the Holy Spirit teaches us and guides us to the truth. When difficult times come we have God's Word and His gift of "peace" to stand on. ~~

Thought for the Day

Jesus' peace is real and present.

But we all, with unveiled face, beholding as in a mirror the glory of the Lord, are being transformed into the same image from glory to glory, just as from the Lord, the Spirit. *2 Corinthians 3:18 NASB*

~~ When the veil has been removed from our faces, the glory of God radiates to the world. A friend was able to witness for Christ when another person told her that they saw peace and love in her face. The friend's answer was "It is not I, it is the Holy Spirit."

The Holy Spirit comes into our hearts when we put aside our personal agendas and Christ becomes the center of our being. Our lives are filled with the glory that comes from loving and serving Jesus. ~~

Thought for the Day

Be a reflection of God's glory.

"In that day you will no longer ask me anything. I tell you the truth, my Father will give you whatever you ask in my name." *John 16:23 NIV*

~~ Jesus knew that the disciples wanted to ask Him a question. Jesus told them that when He was no longer with them they would pray to the Father and He would meet their needs. This is a promise that all of us desperately need to believe: that the Father loves us and through prayer He will hear us and meet all of our needs. ~~

Thought for the Day

Believing in prayer leads to a fruitful Christian life.

We count those blessed who endured. You have heard of the endurance of Job and have seen the outcome of the Lord's dealings, that the Lord is full of compassion and is merciful. *James 5:11 NASB*

~~ Job patiently endured suffering and was blessed by God for his persevering faith. All that Job lost was restored to him because of the Lord's compassion and mercy. We cannot persevere unless we are faced with trials in our lives. There can be no victories without battles. James taught there is a blessing after we have endured. He used Job as an example for us to remember and follow. ~~

Thought for the Day

A blessing follows endurance.

But we have renounced the things hidden because of shame, not walking in craftiness or adulterating the Word of God, but by the manifestation of truth commending ourselves to every man's conscience in the sight of God. *2 Corinthians 4:2 NASB*

~~ Our country, our state, and our hometowns are overflowing with shameful and underhanded practices. God tells us we are to proclaim the truth openly. On a recent Christian television network we were asked, as Christians, to stand up for the Lord - not to lurk in a corner and say, "What can I do?" We can do a lot with the power of the Holy Spirit. We are to get out of our comfort zones and say, "This is wrong according to the Holy Scriptures."

When we meet our Lord face to face, will we have honored our God by professing His truths and standing up for the Word of God? ~~

Thought for the Day

Let us honor God's law.

"In that day you will ask in my name. I am not saying that I will ask the Father on your behalf. No, the Father Himself loves you because you have loved me and have believed that I came from God."
John 16:26-27 NIV

~~ When Jesus was here on earth with His disciples He emphasized that prayer is necessary for us to live full Christian lives. When we pray we are in communication with God.

In the above scripture Jesus is communicating to His disciples that when He was no longer with them to answer their concerns; that they were to pray to the Father in Jesus' name and he would answer because the Father loved them because they loved Jesus.

God loves each of us individually. Communicate with the Father, pray about everything and ask Him to fill your life with His presence and His will. ~~

Thought for the Day

Talk to God – He loves you.

Be of good courage, and He shall strengthen your heart, all you who hope in the Lord. *Psalms 31:24 NKJV*

~~ Hope. When we connect God to the word "hope", it becomes a powerful word.

As followers of Christ we are never to lose hope. Our hope and faith in God will carry us through trials that others might see as hopeless.

Because our hope is in God, He will never abandon us even if we walk away from Him. ~~

Thought for the Day

Never give up.

God is our refuge and strength, a very present help in trouble. Therefore we will not fear, even though the earth be removed, and though the mountains be carried into the midst of the sea.
Psalms 46:1-2 NKJV

~~ We live in a volatile world with threats of more terrorists' attacks on our soil and threats of nuclear warfare.

As Christians we serve a God that is in total control of everything. In these two scriptures we are given the assurance that God is our refuge and strength.

God is our defender; so do not fear the happenings of this world. ~~

Thought for the Day

God is with us.

Therefore, if anyone is in Christ, he is a new creation; the old has gone, the new has come!
2 Corinthians 5:17 NIV

~~ When we become true followers of Christ the old self is left behind. The Holy Spirit fills us with a God-centered self. Our lives are no longer ours because we belong to Christ. Everything is different -- our thoughts, our actions, and our relationships -- when we become God-centered.

When we become a new creation, we strive to do God's will and live our lives to glorify Him. ~~

Thought for the Day

Begin a new life with Him.

For He says, "AT THE ACCEPTABLE TIME I LISTENED TO YOU, AND ON THE DAY OF SALVATIONS I HELPED YOU." Behold, now is "THE ACCEPTABLE TIME," behold, now is the "DAY OF SALVATION." *2 Corinthians 6:2 NASB*

~~ Our time will come when we will stand before God. Christ has offered His salvation to us. In order to receive His salvation we have to commit our hearts to follow Him and live according to His will.

To accept Christ as our personal Savior is the most important decision you will ever make. Have you made your decision to accept Christ as your Savior? Your eternal life depends on it. ~~

Thought for the Day

Without Christ, there is no promise for tomorrow.

There is an appointed time for everything. And there is a time for every event under heaven.
Ecclesiastes 3:1 NASB

~~ When we are walking with God, regardless of the situation that we are in, His timing is perfect and good. The Bible tells us that in all things God works for the good of those who love him, who have been called according to his purpose. He is fulfilling His purpose in us in all the events in our lives, whether joyful or sorrowful. ~~

Thought for the Day

Honor God's timing.

I have not stopped giving thanks for you,
remembering you in my prayers. *Ephesians 1:16 NIV*

~~ Paul continued to pray for the Ephesians. He was
concerned that they did not know enough about Christ. As
believers, we are concerned for those that do not know Him.
Believers and all others can learn more about the life and
message of Christ by studying the Gospels, the first four
books of the New Testament. ~~

Thought for the Day

Knowing Christ is life-changing.

For I am convinced that neither death, nor life, nor angels, nor principalities, nor things present, nor things to come, nor powers, nor height, nor depth, nor any other created thing, will be able to separate us from the love of God, which is in Christ Jesus our Lord. *Romans 8:38-39 NASB*

~~ This Scripture gives us detailed accounts of what cannot separate us from the love of God.

We have God's promise that He loves us and He will never separate Himself from us. God's love is everlasting. His is the only love that we will never lose.

Love is given to us by God. What a wonderful and perfect gift He has given to us. ~~

Thought for the Day

Perfect love is God's love.

Which some have professed and thus gone astray
from the faith. Grace be with you.
1 Timothy 6:21 NASB

~~ Faith is claimed in our hearts by reading God's Word,
praying and trusting God's will for our lives. Faith is
increased when we witness how others deal with conflicts.
Faith is increased every week in church with the prayers,
songs and praises that are given to our Savior. Faith is
increased when we are able to give comfort to someone who
needs comforting.

Our faith will carry us through the best and the worst times.
We nurture our faith to keep it strong and committed to
God.~~

Thought for the Day

Keep your faith God-centered.

Let us not become weary in doing good, for at the proper time we will reap a harvest if we do not give up. *Galatians 6:9 NIV*

~~ Paul is encouraging us to not become weary of doing God's work. Studying God's Word and seeking God in prayer feed our spiritual motivation. Serving God with faith, love and hope will reap a harvest for both God and His followers.

We are to "wait for the Lord" to get the strength we need for each day so that we will never give up doing good for others. ~~

Thought for the Day

Do not be weary of doing good.

"Behold, I stand at the door and knock; if anyone hears My voice and opens the door; I will come in to him and will dine with him, and he with Me."
Revelation 3:20 NASB

~~ Christ is always close by and He knocks and calls out to us. Those who hear His voice and open the door will have Jesus Christ enter their lives.

When we live our lives to serve and please God, He enables us to live a life that is fulfilling to us and pleasing to Him. ~~

Thought for the Day

God leaves it to us to choose to hear His voice.

To God Be the Glory
Psalm 19:1 NIV

Words by Fanny Crosby, music by William Howard Doane, 1875

1. To God be the glory, great things He has done;
So loved He the world that He gave us His Son,
Who yielded His life an atonement for sin,
And opened the life gate that all may go in.

2. O perfect redemption, the purchase of blood,
To every believer the promise of God;
The vilest offender who truly believes,
That moment from Jesus a pardon receives.

3. Great things He has taught us, great things He has done,
And great our rejoicing through Jesus the Son;
But purer, and higher, and greater will be
Our wonder, our transport, when Jesus we see.

Refrain (To be sung after each verse)
Praise the Lord, praise the Lord,
Let the earth hear His voice!
Praise the Lord, praise the Lord,
Let the people rejoice!
O come to the Father, through Jesus the Son,
And give Him the glory, great things He has done.

Thought for Today

Give Him the glory.

"You shall love your neighbor as yourself."
Galatians 5:14b NKJV

~~ Jesus' command to love your neighbor as yourself is not impossible. The ability to obey it without our love for God is impossible. Our love for God will bring the Holy Spirit into our hearts. It is only through the Holy Spirit that we are given love that passes all understanding. Without this love from God we could not love our neighbor as ourselves.

In order for the Holy Spirit to remain in our hearts we need to pray, read His Word and fellowship with other believers. The Holy Spirit enables us to see others as God sees them -- without malice. Our hearts become Christ-like and we want to honor the command to love your neighbor as yourself. ~~

Thought for the Day

To love is to honor God.

That if you confess with your mouth Jesus as Lord, and believe in your heart that God raised Him from the dead, you will be saved. *Romans 10:9 NASB*

~~ The above verse tells us how to become a follower of Christ.   Believe in your heart and confess with your mouth that "Jesus is Lord" and that "God raised Him from the dead," and you will be saved. This is not a complicated process -- salvation is ours when we accept this free gift from God. ~~

Thought for the Day

Seek knowledge of the Word and you will find faith.

Finally, brethren, whatever is true, whatever is honorable, whatever is right, whatever is pure, whatever is lovely, whatever is of good repute, if there is any excellence and if anything worthy of praise, dwell on these things. *Philippians 4:8 NASB*

~~ All of our thoughts are to glorify God. Paul told the Christians to focus their minds on all that is true, noble, right, pure, lovely, admirable, excellent and praiseworthy to the Lord.

This scripture spells out exactly the thoughts that glorify God. When our thoughts are contrary to this scripture then we are not focusing on God. Satan has found a way to enter into our thinking.

Read God's Word and pray for Him to fill your mind and your heart with these truths. ~~

Thought for the Day

Think pure thoughts.

I long to see you so that I may impart to you some spiritual gift to make you strong -- that is, that you and I may be mutually encouraged by each other's faith. *Romans 1:11-12 NIV*

~~ Paul is expressing his love for the people of the church in Rome. He desired to visit the Christians and share his faith and be encouraged by their faith.

We as Christians can receive encouragement from each other because of our mutual faith and our love for God. ~~

Thought for the Day

Encourage each other.

Jesus commented, "Even more blessed are those who hear God's Word and guard it with their lives!"
Luke 11:28 The Message

~~ To honor God's Word is the most important commitment any of us will ever make. Unfortunately, Bible studies and prayer are no longer accepted in our public schools.

Now is the time to stand for God's Word and to guard it as if our lives depended on it. It does. Our choices on earth will help determine where we will spend our eternal lives. ~~

Thought for the Day

To honor God's Word is to be blessed.

Love the LORD your God with all your heart and with all your soul and with all your strength.
Deuteronomy 6:5 NIV

~~ As Christians we are kind and forgiving of others because God is kind and forgiving of us. This is a choice that we are given from God. We can choose to love Him and to love others or to love the world. We cannot have it both ways. We either serve and love God or we serve and love the world.

God is the greatest love we will ever have. Put all your trust in Him and ask Him to fill your heart with His love. ~~

Thought for the Day

God's love has no ending.

Abide in Me, and I in you. As the branch cannot bear fruit of itself unless it abides in the vine, so neither can you unless you abide in Me. I am the vine, you are the branches; he who abides in Me and I in him, he bears much fruit, for apart from Me you can do nothing. *John 15:4-5 NASB*

~~ Abide means to keep in fellowship with Christ so that His life can work in and through us to produce fruit. The branch (Christian believers) cannot produce its own life; it must draw that life from the vine (Jesus Christ). It is our communion with Christ through the Spirit that makes possible the bearing of fruit. Any branch that is not connected to the vine will wither away. ~~

Thought for the Day

Apart from Christ we can do nothing.

We are hard pressed on every side, but not crushed; perplexed, but not in despair; persecuted, but not abandoned; struck down, but not destroyed. *2 Corinthians 4:8-9 NIV*

~~ Without God we can be crushed, despaired and destroyed. Our God gives us hope. Nothing is impossible when we trust and love God.

God is aware of the trials that we go through. He uses the trials to refine and shape us into stronger followers. Without the testing we could never reach the level of faith that God desires for us.

God has carried us through many trials.   He has always been there for us in the past and He will always be there for us in the future. ~~

Thought for the Day

Trust God.

Cultivate inner beauty, the gentle, gracious kind
that God delights in. *1 Peter 3:4 The Message*

~~ Glamour is something that we can put on and take off at
will. Our external beauty, over the years, will decay and
fade away. True inner beauty, which delights God, is real
and internal. Inner beauty is cultivated in the heart and it
does not decay or fade away. Gentle and gracious inner
beauty is the only lasting kind. ~~

Thought for the Day

Beauty comes from the heart.

"Blessed are the poor in spirit, for theirs is the kingdom of heaven." *Matthew 5:3 NASB*

~~ Jesus said these words in His Sermon on the Mount. "Blessed" was a powerful word for the crowds to hear. To the people in the crowd the word meant "divine joy and perfect happiness."

When we put all our faith in Christ we become "blessed" and God's "divine joy and perfect happiness" fill our hearts. ~~

Thought for the Day

Receive God's gift of joy and happiness.

"If anyone wills to do His will, he shall know
concerning the doctrine, whether it is from God, or
whether I speak on My own *authority.*"
John 7:17 NKJV

~~ Spiritual knowledge is given to us when we read and
study God's word. If we have studied God's Word, we will
know when we hear or read false doctrine.

The Bible warns of many false prophets that have appeared
and will appear before Christ's coming.

Without spiritual knowledge we are at risk of falling away
from our faith and losing our eternal life with God. ~~

Thought for the Day

Increase your spiritual knowledge.

Love is patient, love is kind. It does not envy, it does not boast, it is not proud. *1 Corinthians 13:4 NIV*

~~ We will know this kind of love when Christ comes into our hearts. With Christ in our hearts it is possible for us to be patient, kind, not to envy, boast or be proud. Our hearts will be changed with God's grace and love.

With His love we are able to share love that is pleasing to the Lord and edifying to those around us while we expect nothing in return. ~~

Thought for the Day

Share God's love.

Make a clean break with all cutting, backbiting,
profane talk. Be gentle with one another, sensitive.
Forgive one another as quickly and thoroughly as
God in Christ forgave you.
Ephesians 4:31-32 The Message

~~ We grieve the Holy Spirit when we hurt other people.
As Christians, we must be careful because others watch us
to see how we react to conflict. Our conduct can lead others
to Christ or turn them away.

We are commanded to forgive others as Christ has forgiven
us. Forgiving is a gift from God. Let us use that gift to
further God's kingdom. ~~

Thought for the Day

Have a forgiving heart.

I've learned by now to be quite content whatever
my circumstances. I'm just as happy with little as
with much, with much as little. I've found the
recipe for being happy whether full or hungry,
hands full or hands empty.
Philippians 4:11-12 The Message

~~ True contentment can only be found in the Lord. There
will be times in our lives when we go through cycles of low
and high contentment based on the circumstances that
surround us.

In the book of Philippians Paul tells us he found the recipe
for being happy. It is God. When we take Jesus as our Lord
and Savior, contentment is abundant in our lives. ~~

Thought for the Day

Seek contentment from God.

And my God will meet all of your needs according to his glorious riches in Christ Jesus. *Philippians 4:19 NIV*

~~ As children of God we will be provided with all our needs. God is our Father and He desires the best for us. When we are in God's will, we strive to help others that are less fortunate.

Currently we are told we are in a great economic recession. Do not fear because God will always meet the needs of His children. ~~

Thought for the Day

Fear not.

For God did not call us to be impure, but to live a holy life. Therefore, he who rejects this instruction does not reject man but God, who gives you His Holy Spirit. *1 Thessalonians 4:7-8 NIV*

~~ It is becoming more frequent that some Christian leaders are changing the interpretation of the Bible to suit their agendas. The entire Bible is God-breathed and we cannot change any part to justify sin. We cannot decide to follow some of God's commandments; we must follow all of them.

God created marital love between a husband and his wife, a man and a woman. To change God's word is to sin. God's Word is divine and to not honor His word is to reject God.
~~

Thought for the Day

Honor God.

For what will it profit a man if he gains the whole world and forfeits his soul? Or what will a man give in exchange for his soul? For the Son of Man Is going to come in the glory of His Father with His angels, and will then repay every man according to his deeds. *Matthew 16:26-27 NASB*

~~ Believers know that this life is only the beginning and eternal life is granted to those who follow Christ. Those without Christ are unprepared for the next life. Most tend to live life as "this is it," there is no more.

Live your life from an eternal perspective. Christ is returning and when He does, He will review and evaluate everyone's life. Believers and unbelievers will stand before Christ in judgment. He will repay every man according to what he has done or not done with his life. ~

Thought for the Day

Are you prepared to stand before God?

Come back to God Almighty and He'll rebuild your life. *Job 22:23 The Message*

~~ What a wonderful promise we are given. Come back to God Almighty and He'll rebuild our lives. He will -- when we ask Him to show us His will for our lives.

When we turn to God for His comfort and His peace, our lives began to rebuild. God will be there for every step we take. He will never fail us. ~~

Thought for the Day

God never fails His children.

"Be still and know that I am God." *Psalm 46:10 NIV*

~~ God gifts us with life, and only He knows the number of our days. Don't let today or any day end without honoring God.

With all the demands on our time, we must put God at the top of our priority list. It is amazing the result we get when we put God in charge of our lives. It is then that we have the peace and strength to handle the demands of life.

Find a quiet spot, turn off all the electronics and be still and know that He is God. He can and He will carry our burdens because He is God. ~~

Thought for the Day

Be still and exalt God.

But mark this: There will be terrible times in the last days. People will be lovers of themselves, lovers of money, boastful, proud, abusive, disobedient to their parents, ungrateful, unholy, without love, unforgiving, slanderous, without self-control, brutal, not lovers of the good, treacherous, rash, con-ceited, lovers of pleasure rather than lovers of God -- having a form of godliness but denying its power. Have nothing to do with them. *2 Timothy 3:1-5 NIV*

~~ Paul is talking about people who would consider themselves religious. We cannot be lovers of ourselves, lovers of money, boastful, proud, rash, conceited, lovers of pleasure and love God. No, No.

Paul is warning us to have nothing to do with people who have turned their hearts away from God. Putting self first, puts God out of our lives. We cannot serve God first when we are serving ourselves. Let us search our hearts to determine if we are self-centered or God-centered. The answer will determine where we will be in the afterlife. ~~

Thought for the Day

We are in the last days.

The heart of the discerning acquires knowledge; the ears of the wise seek it out. *Proverbs 18:15 NIV*

~~ Living in obedience to God's Word will bring the Holy Spirit to dwell in our hearts. Knowledge from the Word of God will teach us to know when God is speaking to us. Satan will try to speak, but don't be deceived by his words. He is promoting his kingdom here on earth.

Without the Word of God in our hearts, we are unable to make judgments that reflect Godly principles. The above text, "the ears of the wise seek it out," encourages us to seek the facts from all parties involved before any judgment is reached. ~~

Thought for the Day

May all our decisions be God-centered.

The LORD is my shepherd, I shall not be in want. He makes me lie down in green pastures, He leads me beside quiet waters, He restores my soul. He guides me in paths of righteousness for His name's sake. Even though I walk through the valley of the shadow of death, I will fear no evil, for You are with me; Your rod and Your staff, they comfort me. You prepare a table before me in the presence of my enemies. You anoint my head with oil; my cup overflows. Surely goodness and love will follow me all the days of my life, and I will dwell in the house of the LORD forever. *Psalm 23:1-6 NIV*

~~ King David wrote the 23rd Psalm in praise for all the mercies he had received from God. The Great Shepherd that led David is there to lead each of us through the times of our lives. This Psalm is an inspiration, a comfort, an assurance and a blessing to all who call upon God. Surely goodness and love will follow each of us all the days of our lives and we will dwell in the house of the LORD forever. ~~

Thought for the Day

Honor and praise God.

Have no fear of sudden disaster or of the ruin that overtakes the wicked, for the LORD will be your confidence and will keep your foot from being snared. *Proverbs 3:25-26 NIV*

~~ Even when we sleep God is protecting us. We are to put all our confidence in God and know that He is always there for us.

We are to never be fearful because God is God and He is in total control. There is nothing to fear. ~~

Thought for the Day

Do not fear -- God is here.

But He gives a greater grace. Therefore it says, "God is opposed to the proud, but gives grace to the humble." *James 4:6 NASB*

~~ If we love God and dedicate our lives to serving Him, we are not in harmony with the world. It is impossible to serve both God and the world. Make the choice to serve God and to glorify Him. By serving God we oppose the devil, and the attacks will come when least expected. Satan wants us to be proud and have egos that let us think we don't need anyone but ourselves.

When we trust and serve God, He fills our lives with His grace and love. With God's grace there is no room for our egos. Everything that is good comes to us from God. We are nothing on our own. ~~

Thought for the Day

Choose God.

"Here is a simple, rule-of-thumb guide for behavior: Ask yourself what you want people to do for you, then grab the initiative and do it for them. Add up God's law and prophets and this is what you get."
Matthew 7:12 The Message

~~ All of us have heard "Do unto others as you would have them do unto you." This verse is known as "The Golden Rule."

As Christians we follow this great principle because we do not want to hurt others or ourselves. We can only practice this rule with God's love and the Holy Spirit in our hearts.

Practice "The Golden Rule," and in everything let it be to God's glory. This rule is the foundation of active goodness -- just one example of the kind of mercy shown to us every day by our heavenly Father. ~~

Thought For The Day

Reach out to others.

For the sins of their mouths, for the words of their lips, let them be caught in their pride. *Psalm 59:12 NIV*

~~ Only with God's love and grace can our words be uplifting and comforting to those around us. Without God's love and grace, sin can change our words and actions into serving the world instead of God.

Let our thoughts and our actions always edify God and others.

God made each of us and He desires that we love and protect each other -- not to use our words or actions to fall into sin. ~~

Thought For The Day

Beware of sinful pride.

"Because he loves me," says the LORD, "I will rescue him; I will protect him, for he acknowledges my name." *Psalm 91:14 NIV*

~~ My beloved grandfather took me to church before I could walk. In Sunday school I remember singing "Jesus Loves Me." I believed then that Jesus loved me and I still believe.

The Lord has been with me all of my life. He has protected me when I could not protect myself and carried me through times in my life when only His love could save me. It is comforting to know that God watches over us at all times. ~~

Thought For The Day

He is our God. Praise Him.

Trust in Him at all times, you people; pour out your heart before Him; God is a refuge for us.
Psalm 62:8 NKJV

~~ God is our refuge and we can trust Him. Our God has never failed us yet and He never will.

Seek Him, trust Him, pour out your heart to Him and take refuge in Him. ~~

Thought for the Day

God is our refuge in times of trial.

For we brought nothing into this world, and it is
certain we carry nothing out.   *1 Timothy 6:7 NKJV*

~~ At the time of our death, if all our life's work has been to
accumulate things in the world, we will have wasted our
life's work.

Only when we live for and serve Christ will our life's work be
well-lived. ~~

Thought for the Day

Success in this world could lead to failure in the next world.

I Am Healed
Isaiah 53:4-5 NIV

Words and music by Grace Knafel, Copyright, 1975

1. You were wounded for my transgressions
I am healed by your stripes
You were bruised for mine iniquities
I am healed by your stripes
The chastisement of my peace was upon you
Oh yes I'm healed
I am healed; I am healed, by your stripes.

2. Jesus bore my diseases
I am healed by your stripes
Jesus carried all my pains
I am healed by your stripes
You were stricken and afflicted,
Smitten of God for me
I am healed; I am healed by your stripes.
(Repeat both verses)

Thought for the Day

By His stripes, we are healed.

Investigate my life, O God, find out everything
about me; Cross-examine and test me, get a clear
picture of what I'm about; See for yourself whether
I've done anything wrong -- then guide me on the
road to eternal life. *Psalm 139:23-24 The Message*

~~ God is all-knowing. We cannot hide our thoughts, our
actions or anything from God. By reading and studying His
Word, the Holy Spirit will reside in us and our sins will be
revealed.

God loves each of us and He wants the best for us. Let us
ask God to forgive our sins and to guide us to eternal life
with Him. ~~

Thought for the Day

Keep your thoughts and your actions God-centered.

For every creature of God is good. *1 Timothy 4:4 NKJV*

~~ God is good and perfect and everything is good that He creates.

Trust in God who forgives our sins, and let the love and goodness in you flow into the world. ~~

Thought for the Day

Thank God for the good gifts He has given.

Commit to the LORD whatever you do, and your plans will succeed.   *Proverbs 16:3 NIV*

~~ It is best to start each day with praise and trust to the Lord.

As Christians we should recognize every day as God's day -- not just the Sabbath. If we only acknowledge the Lord one day a week we are missing the other six days of praying and seeking our Lord. Start and end every day with the Lord.

God never breaks His promises -- let us not break any to Him. ~~

Thought for the Day

Commit each day to the Lord.

And God will wipe away every tear from their eyes; there shall be no more death, nor sorrow, nor crying. There shall be no more pain, for the former things have passed away. *Revelations 21:4 NKJV*

~~ God promises each of us eternal life with Him without tears or death because Jesus made the sacrifice for us on the cross. There will be no more physical or emotional pain and this world, as we know it, will no longer exist.

Honor God's promises through prayer and faith in Him to secure your reward of eternal life. ~~

Thought for the Day

There is eternal joy for those who love Him.

The Lord has done great things for us, and we are filled with joy. *Psalm 126:3 NIV*

~~ The Israelites were filled with joy because God had ended their seventy years of slavery in Babylon. They were praising God for the great things He had done for them.

The Lord has done great things for you and me. Let our hearts be filled with joy and let us praise our Lord. ~~

Thought for the Day

Give thanks to the Lord.

For man's anger does not bring about the righteous life that God desires. *James 1:20 NIV*

~~ We are unable to do what is right and acceptable to God when we are consumed with anger and wrath. Anger is the opposite of patience. God wants to produce patience in our lives as we mature in Christ. ~~

Thought for the Day

Honor God with our actions.

This is the day the Lord has made; let us rejoice and be glad in it. *Psalm 118:24 NIV*

~~ Our lives are gifts from God. Each life has a beginning and an ending. In between are the days that we are given to live that life.

The Lord has given us this day; let us take the opportunity to do everything possible to bring glory to Him. Let us rejoice and praise God for the salvation He has provided for us in Christ. ~~

Thought for the Day

Celebrate the life God has given you.

But encourage one another day after day, as long as it is still called "Today," so that none of you will be hardened by the deceitfulness of sin.
Hebrews 3:13 NASB

~~ As believers we are instructed to encourage and lift each other up daily with love and concern.

Stay in fellowship with other believers and be strengthened by mutual faith.   God can give us new desires and keep us from falling into sin. ~~

Thought for the Day

Be an encourager for God.

Don't hit back; discover beauty in everyone. If you've got it in you, get along with everybody. Don't insist on getting even; that's not for you to do. "I'll do the judging," says God. "I'll take care of it." *Romans 12:17-19 The Message*

~~ The believer who seeks to serve God will also have enemies. Jesus warned His disciples that their worst enemies might be those of their own household.

This scripture gives us understanding when we are faced with conflict. There is beauty in everyone because God created them. Sometimes, we just have to look a little deeper.

Only God's enduring love and guidance can teach us to love our enemies. Trust in God and remember -- God said, "I'll take care of it." ~~

Thought for the Day

His Word never fails.

Here there is no Greek or Jew, circumcised or uncircumcised, barbarian, Scythian, slave or free, but Christ is all, and is in all. *Colossians 3:11 NIV*

~~ In Christ, there are no designated groups of people, "there is no Greek nor Jew." Christ does not recognize former religious differences, "circumcised or uncircumcised."

Christ does not see any cultural differences, "barbarian or Scythian." In Christ, there are no social positions, "slave or free."

Because we are complete in Christ, there are no earthly differences between people. Joining together, we can have spiritual unity in the Lord. ~~

Thought for The Day

We are all one in Jesus Christ.

Glorify the Lord with me; let us exalt His name together. *Psalm 34:3 NIV*

~~ Praising our Lord is an expression of our love for Him. Knowing Christ and His enduring love for us, should be enough to make us want to glorify the Lord and exalt His name now and forever. ~~

Thought for the Day

Let us glorify the Lord.

May the Lord keep watch between you and me
when we are away from each other. *Genesis 31:49 NIV*

~~ Jacob and Laban did not trust each other, but they
entered into an agreement to not harm the other one. They
requested the Lord to keep watch over them while they
were away from each other. If one harmed the other, God
would know. ~~

Thought for the Day

God knows all.

For the Lord himself will come down from heaven, with a loud command, with the voice of the archangel and with the trumpet call of God, and the dead in Christ will rise first. After that, we who are still alive and are left will be caught up together with them in the clouds to meet the Lord in the air. And so we will be with the Lord forever.
1 Thessalonians 4:16-17 NIV

~~ When Jesus Christ comes down from heaven, there will be three sounds: Jesus' loud command, the voice of the archangel, and the trumpet call of God. Those in the graves, dead in Christ, will hear His voice. The dead will rise first and those who are saved and still alive will be caught up together and they will meet the Lord in the air. This will be the beginning of our forever life with the Lord. ~~

Thought for the Day

There will be a great shout of victory.

There's far more here than meets the eye. The
things we see now are here today, gone tomorrow.
But the things we can't see now will last forever.
2 Corinthians 4:18 The Message

~~ The things we see and feel in the world seem to be real;
but they are only here today and gone tomorrow. They are
not lasting. They are destined to pass away. Only the
eternal things of our spiritual life will last.

By faith and the Word of God we are able to see things that
are invisible. None of us have seen Christ or visited heaven,
yet we know they are real because the Word of God tells us
so. ~~

Thought for the Day

Govern your life with eternal values.

"Unless you do far better than the Pharisees in the matters of right living, you won't know the first thing about entering the kingdom."
Matthew 5:20 The Message

~~ Jesus is telling the crowd that the Pharisees carried out the law but they did not let God into their hearts.

There have been well-known people who have done great deeds, but only later were exposed for behavior that was contrary to God's Word. God wants our hearts to be aligned with Him. When our hearts are right, our deeds will be in harmony with God. ~~

Thought for the Day

Honor God with your thoughts, words and deeds.

The prayer of a righteous man is powerful and effective. *James 5:16b NIV*

~~ The prayer of a righteous man is powerful and effective, but God hears all prayers. It takes time to realize the enormous power of prayer. Prayer should be our first choice and not our last.

Our prayers are our communication with God. When we pray, seeking God and petitioning His will, He hears us. God never fails to answer prayers. Sometimes it is not what we expected, but God's will is the perfect answer. ~~

Thought for the Day

Pray, trust and obey.

Let your conversation be always full of grace,
seasoned with salt, so that you may know how to
answer everyone.   *Colossians 4:6 NIV*

~~ As Christians we have the responsibility to reach out to
the lost around us and help lead them to Christ. When our
opportunity comes to witness, we must make sure our talk
matches our walk. Nothing seems to turn non-believers
away faster than saying one thing but doing another.

Our conversation has to be "seasoned with salt" to have the
substance needed to witness to those around us. This
scripture relays to me that our hearts and speech have to be
pure and filled with God's grace in order to make a
difference to those who listen. ~~

Thought for the Day

Make a difference today.

"This is my command: Love one another the way I loved you. This is the very best way to love. Put your life on the line for your friends. You are my friends when you do the things I command you." *John 15:13-14 The Message*

~~ Jesus died on the cross because of His love for you and me. We can thank God for His amazing love by keeping His commandments and serving Him.

Our friendship and love with God and others will never be perfect, but God's love and friendship is perfect. Let us keep striving to love each other the way God loves us. ~~

Thought for the Day

God is love.

Young men, in the same way be submissive to those who are older. All of you, clothe yourselves with humility toward one another, because, "God opposes the proud but gives grace to the humble."
1 Peter 5:5 NIV

~~ This verse is part of a letter written by Peter to the first century Christians who were going through a time of great trials. Peter's letter was to encourage all believers to submit to God and to each other. The young were instructed to follow the leadership of the older and the older were instructed to listen to the younger.

Jesus gave us a perfect example of submission and humility by washing the feet of His disciples. As a servant of Christ we are to clothe ourselves with humility and serve others. ~~

Thought for the Day

Serving others is to serve God.

Therefore encourage one another and build up one another, just as you also are doing.
1 Thessalonians 5:11 NASB

~~ As followers of Christ we are to love and encourage each other. Our words of kindness and understanding can calm those who are in chaos. We are able to edify each other by praying, studying God's Word, and worshiping together.

We are servants of God and by reaching out and comforting others, we are glorifying God. ~~

Thought for the Day

Encourage and support each other.

For it is only right for me to feel this way about you all, because I have you in my heart, since both in my imprisonment and in the defense and confirmation of the gospel, you all are partakers of grace with me.   *Philippians 1:7 NASB*

~~ Paul had a special place in his heart for the Philippians. During Paul's imprisonment, they sent money and a helper to assist with his ministry. The Philippians shared with Paul God's gracious blessing on his ministry. ~~

Thought for the Day

Share God's blessings with others.

"In this godless world you will continue to experience difficulties. But take heart! I've conquered the world." *John 16:33b The Message*

~~ Godly people are on the outside because they do not conform to the world. Satan goes after godly people -- why waste his time tempting the ones he already controls? Jesus Christ died for our sins and conquered this world.

Let us not be afraid when trials enter our lives, but give all our faith and trust to the Lord. He will handle it. Why can we be so confident? Because God said so. ~~

Thought for the Day

Hang on to God's promises.

For I desire mercy, not sacrifice, and acknowledge-
ment of God rather than burnt offerings.
Hosea 6:6 NIV

~~ Under the old covenant the Israelites honored God
through their sacrifice of burnt offerings and circumcision of
males. Christ died on the cross for our eternal salvation. He
became the ultimate sacrifice for our sins.

Under the new covenant we acknowledge and honor God
through baptism, a public profession of faith. At the Last
Supper, Jesus asked His disciples to eat the bread and drink
the wine "In Remembrance" of Him. When we partake of
the Last Supper we are acknowledging and remembering
God with love, faith and obedience. ~~

Thought for the Day

God desires our love.

However, as it is written: "No eye has seen, no ear has heard, no mind has conceived what God has prepared for those who love Him."
1 Corinthians 2:9 NIV

~~ God has conceived a plan for those who love Him. Our future is secure in Jesus Christ no matter what our circumstances may be.

Here on earth, every day is to be filled with joy even when things are not going along as we hoped or planned. We must always remember whatever circumstances we face, God is present and working for the good of those who love Him. God is present now and will be in the future He has planned for us. ~~

Thought for the Day

We are secure in Christ.

The world is passing away, and also its lusts; but the one who does the will of God lives forever.
1 John 2:17 NASB

~~ Only the faithful servants of God will share the glory of eternal life. Each of us is given a free will. How we choose to use it determines our destiny. Every day, we should strive to know and do the will of God.

Let us stay faithful to God and petition His will for our lives. The world will end but God is eternal. ~~

Thought for the Day

Do not love the world.

You're cheating on God, if all you want is your own way, flirting with the world every chance you get, you end up enemies of God and His way.
James 4:4 The Message

~~ James is warning us to not flirt with the world. "Guard against corruption from the godless world." (*James 1:27 The Message*) We can become involved with the world so gradually that we fall deep into sin.

We have read about famous people that have "flirted with the world." They chose to go their own way and suffered the consequences of sin.

Let us examine our thoughts and our actions to determine if we are faithful to God. Through prayer and the scriptures we can guard against corruption from the world. ~~

Thought for the Day

Be God-Minded.

Why, you do not even know what will happen tomorrow. What is your life? You are a mist that appears for a little while and then vanishes.
James 4:14 NIV

~~ None of us knows what will happen tomorrow, but God does. We do not know what tomorrow will bring, but we know God will be there for us.

We have to prepare for tomorrow by asking God for His will for our lives. God reveals His will to us when we read and study the Bible. Our lives take on a new confidence when we accept Jesus Christ as our Savior. Following His will gives us the courage to face the trials of this world.

Let us invest in this life for an eternal life with God. Don't delay; our lives could be over before we have prepared to stand in judgment before God. ~~

Thought for the Day

Prepare for and invest in eternal life.

God is not a man, that He should lie, nor a son of man, that He should change his mind. Does He speak and then not act? Does He promise and not fulfill? *Numbers 23:19 NIV*

~~ Humans can lie to us; they can change their minds and they can make promises that they never keep. But God in His faithfulness will never lie, never change His mind about His children or make promises that He does not intend to keep.

Only in God can we find forever faithfulness. ~~

Thought for the Day

God is forever faithful.

Your ears will hear a word behind you, "This is the way, walk in it," whenever you turn to the right or to the left.   *Isaiah 30:21 NASB*

~~ If you wander off the road to the right or the left, you will hear His voice behind you saying, "This is the way, walk in it."

Christ speaks to us through His Holy Scriptures. By praying and studying His Word, we will be able to determine what He desires for us to do. ~~

Thought for the Day

Listen for God's voice.

Amazing Praise
Psalm 107:14 NIV

Words and music by Grace Knafel, Copyright, 2005

1. Amazing Praise that fills my heart with gratitude
Amazing Praise I lift my hands to Thee
Amazing Praise has brought me through to victory
He broke the chains and now I am set free.
Chorus
I'll sing my love and all because of Calvary
I'll sing my love to the One who died for me
Amazing Praise has brought me through to victory
He broke the chains and now I am set free.

2. I can't forget the work He did at Calvary
I can't forget once blind but now I see
I can't forget the Son who shed His blood for me
He broke the chains and now I am set free.
Chorus
I'll sing my love and all because of Calvary
I'll sing my love to the One who died for me
Amazing Praise has brought me through to victory
He broke the chains and now I am set free.

Thought for the Day

Because of Him we are free.

Do nothing out of selfish ambition or vain conceit, but in humility consider others better than yourselves. Each of you should look not only to your own interests, but also to the interests of others. *Philippians 2:3-4 NIV*

~~ We were sinners, but by God's grace we are saved. Being united with Christ makes it possible for believers to be like-minded, love each other, and be one in spirit and purpose. We are to guard ourselves from selfishness, prejudice or anything that takes away from unity with God and other believers. ~~

Thought for the Day

Christ is a true example of humility.

If you start thinking to yourselves, "I did all this.
And all by myself. I'm rich. It's all mine!" -- well,
think again. Remember that God, your God, gave
you the strength to produce all this wealth so as to
confirm the covenant that He promised to your
ancestors -- as it is today.
Deuteronomy 8:17-18 The Message

~~ God is the source of every blessing. If we start thinking
that we are the reason for what we have, that the source of
blessings is from us, we have forgotten that God is the true
source of all blessings.

God directed Moses to lead the Israelites from slavery in
Egypt to the Promised Land. The Lord rescued His people
and provided for all their needs during the forty-year
journey. They reached their destination not because of their
own strength or wisdom or because they deserved to live in
a land overflowing with milk and honey. But it was because
of God. He gives us everything we have, just as He gave to
the Israelites. ~~

Thought for the Day

Acknowledge God's blessings.

"Whoever does God's will is my brother and sister and mother." *Mark 3:35 NIV*

~~ Have you ever thought of how Jesus' family felt about Him? It must have been difficult for his siblings to understand that their brother was the Son of God. But Jesus knew who He was and why He was born.

Jesus understood that His natural family was of the flesh. When family members or friends do not meet our expectations we need to reflect on how Jesus would react. Jesus was forgiving and did not let the things of the world change Him or His purpose. Let us always remember we are all brothers and sisters in the family of Christ. ~~

Thought for the Day

We are one family forever in Christ.

They will enter Zion with singing; everlasting joy will crown their heads. Gladness and joy will overtake them, and sorrow and sighing will flee away.   *Isaiah 35:10 NIV*

~~ Only the redeemed will be allowed to enter God's kingdom. Isaiah writes that they will enter Zion with singing. Everlasting joy will crown their heads and gladness and joy will overtake them. There is comfort and joy knowing that all the sorrows in this world will not follow us into God's Kingdom.

God has been keeping His promises to His people for centuries. He will keep His promise to establish His holy kingdom for His believers. In God's Word we will find the faith that gives us victory over the world in this life. ~~

Thought for the Day

Victory is in Jesus.

Be still before the Lord and wait patiently for Him;
do not fret when men succeed in their ways, when
they carry out their wicked schemes. *Psalm 37:7 NIV*

~~ To be still before the Lord and to wait patiently is to
surrender our will and have total faith in God's will and His
timing. God always knows what is best for His followers and
His timing is always perfect.

We are not to fret when men carry out their wickedness but
to remember God's goodness and His justice. God is in total
control and He will judge each of us according to our deeds.
~~

Thought for the Day

God is our judge.

"She will give birth to a son, and you are to give Him the name Jesus, because He will save his people from their sins." *Matthew 1:21 NIV*

~~ Jesus means "Savior". Jesus was born to save his people from their sins. His birth was different from any other child. Mary was His earthly mother but he was born without an earthly father. By the Holy Spirit Jesus was conceived in the womb of Mary, a virgin.

Mary and Joseph, both of the House of David, were engaged. They were referred to as husband and wife. The marriage was not to be consummated until the end of the engagement period. Joseph did not divorce or punish Mary when he found out she was with a child. An angel appeared to Joseph confirming that Mary was to give birth to a son. His name would be Jesus. ~~

Thought for the Day

Jesus is our Savior.

Forget the former things; do not dwell on the past.
Isaiah 43:18 NIV

~~ When God forgives our sins, He forgets them. We are forgiven because of God's mercy and grace. We are to forget the failures of our past and witness for Christ in the present and the future.

God has given us a precious gift -- His forgiveness. All we have to do is ask and put all our faith in Him. ~~

Thought for the Day

God is forever forgiving.

"You can't worship two gods at once. Loving one god, you'll end up hating the other. Adoration of one feeds contempt for the other. You can't worship God and money both."
Matthew 6:24 The Message

~~ We can become enslaved to materialism. It can overtake our hearts, our minds and our will. If we gather material things for ourselves, we will lose them. "Don't hoard treasure down here where it gets eaten by moths and corroded by rust or—worse—stolen by burglars. Stockpile treasure in heaven, where it's safe from moth and rust and burglars. It's obvious, isn't it? The place where your treasure is the place you will most want to be and end up being." (*Matthew 6:19-21 The Message*)

Where is your treasure? Are you using what you have for the glory of God? ~~

Thought for the Day

Align your heart with God.

Jesus said, "I am the Road, also the Truth, also the Life. No one gets to the Father apart from me. If you really knew me, you would know my Father as well. From now on, you do know Him. You've even seen Him!" *John 14:6-7 The Message*

~~ Jesus is our "Road" to the Father. There is no other way to travel except the road with Jesus that leads to God. The "Truth " is Jesus leading us to God and His promises. We were promised a Savior and God gave us Jesus. Jesus is the "Life." We give our lives to Jesus and we are with Him now and forever.

Jesus is both God and man. He told his followers "If you really knew me, you would know my Father as well." Jesus was letting them know that because they had seen Him, they had also seen the Father. ~~

Thought for the Day

Jesus is the Way, the Truth and the Life.

"You will seek me and find me when you seek me with all your heart." *Jeremiah 29:13 NIV*

~~ It is our responsibility to seek God. We communicate with God through His presence, through prayer and through God's grace.

We are not promised that we will be spared from suffering or hardships. But we are promised that nothing can separate us from God. ~~

Thought for the Day

Seek God wholeheartedly.

But blessed is the man who trusts in the Lord,
whose confidence is in Him. *Jeremiah 17:7 NIV*

~~ We are blessed and strengthened when we trust in God.
"He will be like a tree planted by the water that sends out its
roots by the stream, it does not fear when heat comes; its
leaves are always green. It has no worries in a year of
drought and never fails to bear fruit." (*Jeremiah 17:8 NIV*)

With all our faith in the Lord, there is no room for fear. He
will keep watch over those who are faithful. ~~

Thought for the Day

Plant your faith in the Lord.

Keep your eyes open, hold tight to your convictions, give it all you've got, be resolute, and love without stopping. *1 Corinthians 16:14 The Message*

~~ This Scripture is part of a letter that Paul wrote to the church in Corinth. Paul was concerned that there would be further division in the church. His instructions were to keep their eyes open, stand firm in their faith, give all they have to give and be resolute. Paul instructed the Corinthians to be strong but to add love and kindness to everything they did.

As we wait for Christ to return, we should follow the same instructions that Paul wrote to the Corinthians almost two centuries ago. God's Word never goes out of date. ~~

Thought for the Day

Keep Christ close.

So let God work His will in you. Yell a loud No to the devil and watch him scamper. *James 4:7 The Message*

~~ King David committed adultery with Bathsheba and he put her husband, who was in David's army, on the front line. David hid his sins for almost a year before confessing them to God. Only upon David's unconditional surrender to God, did he experience peace and joy.

Unconditional surrender to God is the only way to have victory. Surrendering our will to God is asking for His will to be done, not ours. Being inside of God's will, Satan will flee from us. ~~

Thought for the Day

We must surrender our wills.

Because of the Lord's great love we are not consumed, for His compassions never fail.
Lamentations 3:22 NIV

~~ God knows our emotions. We were created in His image. He feels our pain and suffering because of His great love for each of us. The Lord does not give us more than we can handle. Trust Him and He will give you the strength to go through all the storms in your life.

Call out to the Lord. He will never fail you or forsake you. ~~

Thought for the Day

Trust God in everything.

"You shall have no other gods before me."
Exodus 20:3 NIV

~~ This is the first commandment that God dictated to Moses on Mount Sinai. God emphasized this commandment more than the other nine. We must honor the first commandment or we are separated from God.

Thought for the Day

Worship only the Lord your God.

Consider it pure joy, my brothers, whenever you face trials of many kinds, because you know that the testing of your faith develops perseverance. Perseverance must finish its work so that you may be mature and complete, not lacking anything.
James 1:2-4 NIV

~~ In the first chapter of James we are instructed that through faith in Christ we can experience victory. The result of this victory is spiritual maturity. James continues in Chapter one to give us four essentials for victory in trials: a joyful attitude, an understanding mind, a surrendered will, and a heart that wants to believe.

Peter said, "Friends, when life gets really difficult, don't jump to the conclusion that God isn't on the job. Instead, be glad that you are in the very thick of what Christ experienced. This is a spiritual refining process, with glory just around the corner." (*1 Peter 4:12-14 The Message*) ~~

Thought for the Day

Christ is faithful.

Pray continually; give thanks in all circumstances, for this is God's will for you in Christ Jesus.
1 Thessalonians 5:17-18 NIV

~~ Giving thanks to God is a vital part in worshiping God. "Let the word of Christ dwell in you richly in all wisdom, teaching and admonishing one another in psalms and hymns and spiritual songs, singing with grace in your hearts to the Lord." (*Colossians 3:16 NKJV*) Each of us has an abundance of gifts that God has given us. Think about it and give thanks to God. ~~

Thought for the Day

Worship God through prayer and thanksgiving.

The Pharisees and religious scholars asked, "Why do your disciple's flout the rules, showing up at meals without washing their hands?"
Mark 7:5 The Message

~~ The next three verses in Mark give us Jesus' reply to their question. Jesus answered, "Isaiah was right about frauds like you, hit the bull's eye in fact: these people make a big show of saying the right thing, but their heart isn't in it. They act like they are worshiping me, but they don't mean it. They just use me as a cover for teaching whatever suits their fancy, ditching God's command and taking up the latest fads." (*Mark 7:6-8 The Message*) Jesus called them frauds because their hearts were away from God.

In the Sermon on the Mount, Jesus stressed that true holiness is inward affection and attitude and not just what we do and with whom we associate. In other words, our hearts have to be pure. ~~

Thought for the Day

Let our hearts be pure in God.

Trust God from the bottom of your heart; don't try to figure out everything on your own. Listen for God's voice in everything you do, everywhere you go; He's the one who will keep you on track.
Proverbs 3:5-6 The Message

~~ Trusting God from the bottom of your heart does not mean that you stop thinking.

We should love the Lord with our minds as well as our hearts.

We need to seek God's will in everything we do. His will is revealed in the Word of God, the only way to know His will is to study His Word and obey. Let us not lean on our own understanding and thereby miss God's will for our life.

God's plan for us is good, pleasing and perfect. If we trust the Lord, we will be on track. ~~

Thought for the Day

Seek God in everything.

"It is God who arms me with strength and makes my way perfect." *2 Samuel 22:33 NIV*

~~ When we are armed with God's strength, we are empowered for victory. There is always victory when we seek the mind of God. In life there are many challenges; let God arm you with His strength and His love. ~~

Thought for the Day

God will make your way perfect.

Do not merely listen to the Word, and so deceive yourselves. Do what it says. Anyone who listens to the Word but does not do what it says is like a man who looks at his face in a mirror and, after looking at himself, goes away and immediately forgets what he looks like. *James 1:22-24 NIV*

~~ When we look into the mirror of God's Word we will see ourselves as we really are if we look deep enough. We also must remember and practice what the Word tells us. Reading and studying the Word should not be something that is carelessly done. We must look deep into our own hearts and remember that it takes time, attention and sincere devotion to live in the light of God's Word. ~~

Thought for the Day

Be a listener and a doer of God's Word.

"When these things begin to take place, stand up and lift your heads, because your redemption is drawing near." *Luke 21:28 NIV*

~~ There will be wars and commotions. Nations will rise against a nation, kingdom against kingdom. There will be great earthquakes and famines. We are told in Luke that when these things begin to take place, the time of Christ's return is drawing near. We are to live a holy and godly life while we await our Savior's return.

There are those who do not believe that Christ will return. Christ has promised He will return and will keep His promise to establish a new heaven and a new earth for the righteous. ~~

Thought for the Day

Always be on watch, and pray.

As iron sharpens iron, so one man sharpens another. *Proverbs 27:17 NIV*

~~ A good friend is a gift from God. God can continue to do amazing things in our lives through dear friends. Best friends can nurture and encourage us through our trials and challenges.

Friendship is one of the original gifts from God. God made Adam and He saw that man should not be alone. God created Eve and this union was the first marriage, but they were also best friends. I believe God gives us people to accompany us through seasons of our lives. As iron sharpens iron, good friendships sharpen and strengthen us. ~~

Thought for the Day

A good friend is an amazing gift.

For the wages of sin is death, but the gift of God is eternal life in Christ Jesus our Lord.   *Romans 6:23 NIV*

~~ When serving a master, you are given wages. Sin pays wages and the result is eternal life without God. Wages given from serving God is eternal life. We are free to choose which master we wish to serve, but we will not be able to change the consequences of our choice.

Think about your choices now before it is too late. The gift of God is eternal life in Christ Jesus our Lord. ~~

Thought for the Day

Choose Christ.

Anyone who meets a testing challenge head-on and manages to stick it out is mighty fortunate. For such persons loyally in love with God, the reward is life and more life. *James 1:12 The Message*

~~ Because we love God, we face testing with a joyful attitude. Testing is a challenge but we know God loves us and He is there to guide us step by step. Where there is love there is surrender and obedience.

The Christian who loves God, and who knows that God loves him, will not fall apart when God permits trials to come. He is secure in God's love. ~~

Thought for the Day

We are secure in God's love.

But whoever listens to me will live in safety and be at ease, without fear of harm. *Proverbs 1:33 NIV*

~~ How we respond to God's message is a matter of life or death. It is impossible for us to decide not to decide. Being neutral does not work. God tells us that whoever listens to Him will live in safety and without fear.

There is wisdom in God's truth. Wisdom calls us to a life changing decision that turns us away from sin and turns us to Christ. Those who reject God's wisdom sin against their own souls. Rejecting God's truth puts us on a path to eternal death without God. ~~

Thought for the Day

Listen to God's wisdom.

Watch what God does, and then do it, like children
who learn proper behavior from their parents.
Mostly what God does is love you. Keep company
with Him and learn a life of love. Observe how
Christ loved us. His love was not cautious but
extravagant. He didn't love in order to get
something from us but to give everything of himself
to us. Love like that. *Ephesians 5:1-2 The Message*

~~ God loves us as He loved His Son. Because He loves us,
He let His Son die on the cross for our salvation. Love is the
greatest of virtues in a Christian's life. We can express our
love for God by living a life that is pleasing and acceptable to
the Father. Love other people as well as you do yourself.
We can never go wrong when we love God and others. ~~

Thought for the Day

Love as God loves.

Bear with each other and forgive whatever
grievances you may have against one another.
Forgive as the Lord forgave you. *Colossians 3:13 NIV*

~~ As Christians we are to forgive as quickly and completely
as God has forgiven us. Not only are we to forgive but also
we cannot retaliate against that person. If we do not
forgive someone, feelings of malice develop in our hearts.
These feelings can lead to even greater sin.

It is Christ-like to forgive and forgiveness opens our hearts
to the fullness of God's love. It is only with God's love that
we can forgive those who trespass against us. ~~

Thought for the Day

Forgive as the Lord forgives.

The Lord appeared to him from afar, saying, "I have loved you with an everlasting love; Therefore I have drawn you with lovingkindness." *Jeremiah 31:3 NASB*

~~ Has your life not gone the way you planned? Have you ever been so discouraged you wanted to give up? God's everlasting love is the answer. He never gives up on us regardless of what we have done or how we have lived our lives.

Let God take care of you, let Him be your guide on your journey to eternal life with Him. ~~

Thought for the Day

Let God enable you to cope with life.

Then Your Light Shall Break Forth Like The Morning
Isaiah 58:8-10 NIV

Words and music by Grace Knafel, Copyright, 2005

1. Then your light shall break forth like the morning,
And your healing shall spring forth speedily,
Your righteousness shall go on before you;
And the glory of the LORD shall be your guard

2. Then you will call and the LORD will answer
The Lord will hear your cry for help
If you do away with the yoke of oppression
Then your night will become like the noonday.

3. Then your light shall break forth like the morning,
And your healing shall spring forth speedily,
Your righteousness shall go on before you;
And the glory of the LORD shall be your guard

4. Then I will call and the LORD will answer
The LORD will hear my cry for help
If I do away with the yoke of oppression
Then my night will become like the noonday.

Thought for the Day

Call on the LORD for your help.

Then David said to Nathan, "I have sinned against the Lord." Nathan replied, "The Lord has taken away your sin. You are not going to die. But because by doing this you have made the enemies of the Lord show utter contempt, the son born to you will die." *2 Samuel 12:13-14 NIV*

~~ David suffered the consequences of his sin. God forgave King David for adultery with Bathsheba and for having her husband killed. His sins were forgiven but God's judgment was that his son with Bathsheba would die. God forgives us, but He does not eliminate all the consequences that come with sin.

The consequences of sin affect not only us, but also those we know and love. ~~

Thought for the Day

Sin has consequences.

Bear one another's burdens, and so fulfill the law of Christ. *Galatians 6:2 NKJV*

~~ The word "burdens" indicates that the burden is heavy and difficult to carry. The Spirit-led Christian desires to help lift the burdens of others. When we love, encourage and help others to overcome their burdens we are fulfilling the "law of love" which fulfills the "law of Christ."

Let us reach out to others with love. ~~

Thought for the Day

Put the other person first.

Then you will know which way to go, since you have never been this way before. *Joshua 3:4a NIV*

~~ In our lifetime we must expect and prepare to pass ways that we have not passed before. We will know the way to go when we put aside all our fear and put all our faith and trust in God. Worshiping God and studying His Word nurture our faith.

God knows the way and He is our protector. We will never be lost as long as we put away sin and trust God to lead us to Him. ~~

Thought for the Day

Let God lead you to Him.

If your heart is broken, you'll find God right there; if you're kicked in the gut, He'll help you catch your breath. *Psalm 34:18 The Message*

~~ The righteous are not spared from the pain of grief, loss, sorrow, failure and the many other problems in this world. But, we are promised that if we trust Him and call on Him, the Lord will see us through our troubles.

God promises to be close to the brokenhearted. He gives us courage, wisdom and power to endure any circumstances in our lives. ~~

Thought for the Day

God is divine power.

"If someone forces you to go one mile, go with him two miles." *Matthew 5:41 NIV*

~~ The Roman soldiers forced Simon the Cyrene to carry Jesus' cross. Believers bear their crosses by doing the things He asks us to do, that we can only do through His Grace. We are not forced to serve like Simon; we do it for God and to His Glory. ~~

Thought for the Day

We willingly carry our crosses.

For God did not give us a spirit of timidity, but a spirit of power, of love and of self-discipline.
2 Timothy 1:7 NIV

~~ God has not given us the spirit of fear, but the spirit of power, of love and of self-discipline. These things are in us because of the Holy Spirit

It is the Holy Spirit who enables us to serve God, and through Him we can overcome fear and bear whatever comes to us. ~~

Thought for the Day

Our strength and power are from God.

Do not forget to entertain strangers, for by so doing some people have entertained angels without knowing it. *Hebrews 13:2 NIV*

~~ Moses (*Genesis 18*) gives the story of Abraham showing generous hospitality to the Lord and two of His angels. Abraham did not know who they were when he welcomed them; it was only later that he discovered their identities.

Where there is true Christian love, there will also be hospitality. This was an important ministry in the early church. Many believers were driven out of their homes because of persecution. The churches met in homes, so believers would stay with the host. You and I may never entertain angels, but any stranger could be a blessing to us. ~~

Thought for the Day

Christian love = hospitality.

Do not repay evil with evil or insult with insult, but with blessing, because to this you were called so that you may inherit a blessing.   *1 Peter 3:9 NIV*

~~ Not only are we to love God's people but we are to love our enemies. We can love our enemies only when God's love fills our hearts. We are to follow Jesus' example and return good for evil. As God's children we have to show mercy to those who hurt us. This is how God deals with us. He shows us mercy.

As Christians we are *called* to love our enemies and do them good when they treat us badly. We are also *called* to "inherit a blessing." The persecutions we experience on earth today only add to our blessed inheritance of glory when we go to heaven. When we treat our enemies with love and mercy, we also receive a blessing. ~~

Thought for the Day

Depend on prayer and God's power.

But thanks be to God, who always leads us in triumphal procession in Christ and through us spreads everywhere the fragrance of the knowledge of him.   *2 Corinthians 2:14 NIV*

~~ Paul is praising God. Even though Paul had many problems and detours in his ministry, he always knew that God was in control.

Jesus Christ came to earth and completely defeated Satan. Christ was triumphant in saving lost souls who had been in bondage. What a victory! Because Jesus Christ overcame, there will always be victory over any tragedy. Our faith in God will lead us in triumphal procession in Christ. ~~

Thought for the Day

Our faith leads to God.

For with you is the fountain of life; in your light we see light.   *Psalm 36:9 NIV*

~~ True happiness comes from God, the fountain of life. Life and light go together, and the Lord is the source of both. The righteous are given the Lord's rich blessings. God has given us life and the light to guide us to Him and eternal life. ~~

Thought for the Day

God is our fountain of life.

For the joy of the Lord is your strength.
Nehemiah 8:10 NIV

~~ We can find Christian joy by believing what God says in His Word and acting upon it. Our faith has to be based on God's Word. This faith will give us joy that will take us through all the problems of life.

As God's followers we will have burdens, but we also experience power that transforms our sorrow into joy. For the joy of the Lord is our strength. ~~

Thought for the Day

True joy is of the Lord.

For our struggle is not against flesh and blood, but against the rulers, against the authorities, against the powers of this dark world and against the spiritual forces of evil in the heavenly realms.
Ephesians 6:12 NIV

~~ Our battle, as believers, is not with flesh and blood. Our battle is with demons. We are up against a powerful army wanting to defeat Christ's church. Satan does everything in his power to turn us away from God.

By His death and resurrection Christ overcame the world, and the flesh and the devil. As believers, we do not fight *for* victory -- we fight *from* victory. Satan is a strong enemy and only with the power of God can we stand against him. ~~

Thought for the Day

Believers walk in victory.

"In my Father's house are many rooms; if it were not so, I would have told you. I am going there to prepare a place for you." *John 14:2 NIV*

~~ For believers, heaven is a real place. Heaven is where God dwells and where Jesus sits at the right hand of the Father. In heaven there will be no death, sorrow, crying or pain. What a wonderful place heaven will be and it will be our home forever. ~~

Thought for the Day

Heaven is God's home.

A life devoted to things is a dead life, a stump; a God-shaped life is a flourishing tree.
Proverbs 11:28 The Message

~~ When we dedicate our lives to riches, we are living dead lives. We are not living the life that God intended for us. God wants to be in our hearts and in our spirit. A God-shaped life is alive and flourishing like a tree that has deep roots. A God-shaped believer lives a life that is pleasing to God.

We must ask ourselves -- what is the most important thing in our lives? If it is not God, then we are not living a God-shaped life. Are you living a dead life or a God-shaped life? ~~

Thought for the Day

A God-shaped life is forever.

Create in me a pure heart, O God, and renew a steadfast spirit within me. *Psalm 51:10 NIV*

~~ King David had sinned by taking another man's wife and having her husband killed. David's sins affected his whole being. He called out to God for more cleansing. He wanted his entire being to be restored so that he could serve the Lord with a pure heart. David asked the Lord to create a new heart within him and renew a steadfast spirit that would not waver.

David was incapable of changing his own heart and renewing his own spirit. Only God can create a pure heart and renew a steadfast spirit. Let us ask God to create in us a pure heart and a renewed steadfast spirit. ~~

Thought for the Day

Only God can change hearts.

Better a poor man whose walk is blameless than a
rich man whose ways are perverse. Proverbs 28:6 NIV

~~ A righteous poor man who lives according to the Word
of God and obeys God's commandments is richer than the
perverse rich man. The poor man's riches are not on earth
but stored in heaven with God. The blameless righteous
man will inherit eternal life. The rich man pretends to be
righteous and truthful but his heart is sinful. On judgment
day he will not be blameless.

The decisions we make in life will determine whether or not
God finds us blameless. ~~

Thought for the Day

Live to be blameless.

For this reason, since the day we heard about you, we have not stopped praying for you and asking God to fill you with the knowledge of His will through all spiritual wisdom and understanding. And we pray this in order that you may live a life worthy of the Lord and may please Him in every way: bearing fruit in every good work, growing in the knowledge of God, being strengthened with all power according to His glorious might so that you may have great endurance and patience, and joyfully giving thanks to the Father, who has qualified you to share in the inheritance of the saints in the kingdom of light. *Colossians 1:9-12 NIV*

~~ Paul had never met the Colossians, but he faithfully prayed for them. Paul's prayers were written in letters from prison. He was aware of the false teachings that were threatening the church. Paul prayed for spiritual intelligence, practical obedience and moral excellence, which lead to spiritual power.

Spiritual power gives us patience to endure suffering with thanksgiving. It also qualifies us to share in the inheritance of the saints in God's kingdom of light. ~~

Thought for the Day

Prayer is powerful.

Man does not live on bread alone but on every word that comes from the mouth of the Lord.
Deuteronomy 8:3b NIV

~~ Jesus had been in the desert fasting for forty days and forty nights. Jesus was hungry and the devil tried to get Him to turn stones into bread. Jesus answered the devil by telling him that man does not live on bread alone, but on every Word that comes from the mouth of God. ~~

Thought for the Day

God's Word is the bread of life.

For the Word of God is living and active. Sharper than any double-edged sword, it penetrates even to dividing soul and spirit, joints and marrow; it judges the thoughts and attitudes of the heart.
Hebrews 4:12 NIV

~~ God knows our hearts. He uses His Word to enable us to see the sin and unbelief in our own hearts. That is why each of us must study the Word of God, so we can see ourselves as we really are. We can accomplish this by listening to His Word, understanding it, trusting it and obeying it. ~~

Thought for the Day

The Word of God lives.

Therefore, as we have opportunity, let us do good to all people, especially to those who belong to the family of believers. *Galatians 6:10 NIV*

~~ Paul encouraged the Galatians to keep on doing good to all people, but especially to the family of believers. Let us also be encouraged to keep on doing good for others even if we feel it is not appreciated. Let us trust in God for the results of our good deeds. ~~

Thought for the Day

Let our works be pleasing to God.

So, chosen by God for this new life of love, dress in the wardrobe God picked out for you: compassion, kindness, humility, quiet strength, discipline. Be even-tempered, content with second place, quick to forgive an offense. Forgive as quickly and comp- letely as the Master forgave you. And regardless of what else you put on, wear love. It's your basic, all-purpose garment. Never be without it.
Colossians 3:14 The Message

~~ Love is the most important of the Christian virtues. Love binds all the other virtues together. All of the spiritual qualities that Paul named are aspects of true Christian love. We honor God by dressing in the wardrobe God picked out for His believers.

Let love rule in your life and all of these spiritual virtues will bring beauty and harmony into your life. Harmony promotes spiritual maturity. All of these virtues keep our lives balanced and growing. ~~

Thought for the Day

Choose God's virtues.

So let's keep focused on that goal, those of us who want everything God has for us. If any of you have something else in mind, something less than total commitment, God will clear your blurred vision -- you'll see it yet! Now that we're on the right track, let's stay on it. *Philippians 3:15-16 The Message*

~~ We are to keep our focus on God. What matters most is what God thinks about our focus, not what the world thinks. It is impossible for any believer to live a perfect Christian life. But, the Holy Spirit will empower us to press on and to honor our commitment to God. ~~

Thought for the Day

Get a focus check-up.

You will keep in perfect peace Him whose mind is steadfast, because He trusts in you. *Isaiah 26:3 NIV*

~~ Only through our steadfast faith in God, can we find perfect peace. *Isaiah 32:17, NIV*, reads "The fruit of righteousness will be peace, the effect of righteousness will be quietness and confidence forever."

When we are devoted to God, we receive His unchanging love and His power. Armed with His love and His power we are able to live in a world of chaos and not lose God's perfect peace. ~~

Thought for the Day

Seek God's perfect peace.

"For with God nothing shall be impossible."
Luke 1:37 NKJV

~~ Gabriel appeared to Mary, a virgin, to explain that she would give birth to the Son of God. Nothing is impossible with God. The angel ended his message by telling Mary that her aged-relative, Elizabeth, was going to have a child. Elizabeth was well past the childbearing age, but with God nothing is impossible.

There is nothing in my life or yours that is impossible for God. Whatever we face, remember that God can do the impossible. We only have to put all our faith and trust in Him. I know, because God has done things in my life that I first thought were impossible. They were impossible for me, but not for God. ~~

Thought for the Day

With God all things are possible.

"Woe to me!" I cried. "I am ruined! For I am a man of unclean lips, and I live among a people of unclean lips, and my eyes have seen the King, the Lord Almighty." *Isaiah 6:5 NIV*

~~ Isaiah saw the Lord and he heard the angels praising God. He realized that he was unclean. His lips were touched by a live burning coal. God then told Isaiah that his sins were forgiven. Isaiah responded by totally submitting himself to God's service.

Before we accept God's call to speak for Him to others, we must be cleansed as Isaiah was. We must confess our sins and let God take total control of our lives. We must be purified so that we can truly represent God, who is pure and holy. ~~

Thought for the Day

God is pure and holy.

Woe to those who call evil good and good evil, who put darkness for light and light for darkness, who put bitter for sweet and sweet for bitter.
Isaiah 5:20 NIV

~~ Only in the Word of God can we find the true definition of sin. Beware of those in the world that call evil good and good evil. There are consequences for sin regardless of how it is presented to us. Let the Word of God, the Bible, be our guide for making moral choices. ~~

Thought for the Day

Beware of deception.

This is the confidence we have in approaching God: that if we ask anything according to His will, He hears us. And if we know that He hears us -- whatever we ask -- we know that we have what we asked of Him. *1 John 5:14-15 NIV*

~~ When Jesus was on earth, He reached out and helped many people. Does He still help people? Yes. We can have total confidence when we pray because His Word tells us that if we ask anything according to His will, He hears us. God knows what is best for each of us. He knows our past, present and future.

Asking that God's will and not our will be done com-municates to our Father that we have put all our faith and trust in Him. He will hear us and He will give us a definite answer. ~~

Thought for the Day

Pray with confidence.

"This then, is how you should pray." *Matthew 6:9a NIV*

~~ Jesus gave to His disciples a prayer known as "The Lord's Prayer." This prayer was given to the disciples and us as an example of how to pray. One of the many purposes of prayer is to glorify God's name and to ask for His help to accomplish His will on earth.

Let us pray The Lord's Prayer, "Our Father in heaven, hallowed be Your name, Your kingdom come, Your will be done on earth as it is in heaven. Give us today our daily bread. Forgive us our debts, as we also have forgiven our debtors. And lead us not into temptation, but deliver us from the evil one" ~~

Thought for the Day

Thy will be done.

Let the glory of the Lord endure forever.
Psalm 104:31 NASB

~~ Because God created each of us; He is worthy of our praising and glorifying Him forever.

Let us glorify the Lord with our own bodies and minds, our talents and possessions. We should gratefully accept all He has given us and use it to glorify Him. ~~

Thought for the Day

Let us rejoice in God's creation.

He Is Like No Other God
Psalm 147:4,8,11 NIV

Words and music by Grace Knafel, Copyright, 2005

Chorus to be sung first and after every verse.
He is like no other God
He is like no other King
He's ruler of the universe
He's master over everything

1. And our God is a mighty God
There is nothing that He cannot do
And our God is an awesome King
He rules over everything
And our God He delights in those
Who trust in His unfailing love

2. And our God fills the sky with clouds
He supplies all the earth with rain
And our God counts the number of stars
He calls them each by name
And our God makes the grass to grow
To provide the food in the field

(Ending) And His name is Jesus, And His name is Jesus.

Thought for the Day

God can do everything but fail.

It is better to take refuge in the Lord than to trust in man. *Psalms 118:8 NIV*

~~ There is no future in trusting man for your salvation. Only trusting our lives to God leads us to eternal life with Him. God will bless those who take refuge in Him. ~~

Thought for the Day

Put your trust in God.

The Lord Himself goes before you and will be with you; He will never leave you nor forsake you. Do not be afraid; do not be discouraged.
Deuteronomy 31:8 NIV

~~ The Lord has gone before us, but He has given us the Holy Bible to guide us. The Hebrews fleeing from Egypt did not have the Bible. So God gave them a pillow of cloud and a pillar of fire so they would know that God was always there and always watching over them as they traveled to the Promised Land.

As the Hebrews were guided by the cloud and the fire, believers are guided by God's Word on their journey to eternal life. His Word promises believers that He will never leave nor forsake them. Never be afraid or discouraged for God is with you. ~~

Thought for the Day

God is our trusted guide.

Make sure that nobody pays back wrong for wrong, but always try to be kind to each other and to everyone else.   *1 Thessalonians 5:15 NIV*

~~ Often when we reach out to help others, they reject us and even oppose us. We cannot become discouraged or repay wrong for wrong. Our goal should be to serve with the love of Christ.

We are to be careful to do what is right in the eyes of everybody. As believers, we are to live at peace with everyone around us, even if they are not peaceful. God's Word directs us to not take revenge but leave it in God's hands. ~~

Thought for the Day

Serve Christ in everything.

Not only so, but we also rejoice in our sufferings, because we know that suffering produces perseverance; perseverance, character; and character, hope. *Romans 5:3-4 NIV*

~~ As believers, trials work for us not against us. There is no amount of suffering that can separate us from the Lord. Trials and suffering draw us closer to the Lord and our character becomes more like His.

Both nonbelievers and believers have suffering in their lives, but believers put their hope in Christ. Christ has promised us that there will be no suffering or trials for those that inherit eternal life with Him. ~~

Thought for the Day

Let us thank God for opportunities to grow.

Then He called the crowd to Him along with His disciples and said: "If anyone would come after me, he must deny himself and take up his cross and follow me. For whoever wants to save his life will lose it, but whoever loses his life for me and for the gospel will save it." *Mark 8:34-35 NIV*

~~ Jesus used the image of the cross to describe how we must deny ourselves in order to follow Him. He taught His disciples and the crowds that gathered around Him that there is a price to pay for being a true follower. ~~

Thought for the Day

Take up your cross and follow Christ.

You've all been to the stadium and seen the athlete's race. Everyone runs; one wins. Run to win. All good athletes train hard. They do it for a gold medal that tarnishes and fades. You're after one that's gold eternally.
1 Corinthians 9:24-25 The Message

~~ Serving Christ takes discipline and stamina. Are you willing to discipline yourself to find time in your busy schedule to study God's Word and to worship Him? As Christians, we do not run the race to get to heaven. We are in the race because we have been saved through faith in Jesus Christ.

The gold medals we are given here on earth will tarnish and fade but the gold medal (eternal life) that God will give His believers will last forever. ~~

Thought for the Day

Are you willing to serve Christ?

Let no debt remain outstanding, except the
continuing debt to love one another, for he who
loves his fellowman has fulfilled the law.
Romans 13:8 NIV

~~ The basic principle of the Christian life is to love one
another. We are to love others as Christ loves each of us.
This love will help bring unbelievers to Christ.

Jesus walked on earth and was a living example of God's
love. Let us strive to be living examples of Jesus' everlasting
love. ~~

Thought for the Day

Reach out with love.

Therefore, there is now no condemnation for those who are in Christ Jesus. *Romans 8:1 NIV*

~~ Even those who are in Christ Jesus make mistakes and sin. Abraham lied about his wife; David committed adultery; Peter tried to kill a man with his sword. They all had to face the consequences because of their sins, but they did not suffer condemnation.

In Christ, there is no condemnation. He has offered us freedom from sin. ~~

Thought for the Day

In Christ Jesus there is freedom from sin.

"And when two or three of you are together because of me, you can be sure that I'll be there."
Matthew 18:20 The Message

~~ Jesus knew that the time would come that He would not
be present with His followers in body. Christ's Holy Spirit is
present when two or three sincere believers meet to pray.
When they pray, they are to ask that God's will be done, not
their will.

They will be heard and their prayers will be answered. ~~

Thought for the Day

Meet with others to pray.

And so we know and rely on the love God has for us. God is love. Whoever lives in love lives in God, and God in him. *1 John 4:16 NIV*

~~ In the Bible there are many Scriptures regarding God's love for us. The more we understand His love, the easier it is to obey Him and to love others.

God's love for us is unfailing. God is love. Believers who love their fellow man live in God and God in them. Our spiritual life grows when we live in love. ~~

Thought for the Day

God is love.

He who fears the Lord has a secure fortress, and for his children it will be a refuge. *Proverbs 14:26 NIV*

~~ He who fears the Lord sets up a secure fortress for himself and his children. When our priorities are on God, we are living a God-centered life and we can find refuge in Him. ~~

Thought for the Day

In the Lord we are secure.

"For whoever gives you a cup of water to drink in my name, because you belong to Christ, assuredly, I say to you, he will by no means lose his reward."
Mark 9:41 NKJV

~~ When we share what we have, even a cup of cool water, we are showing our love for Christ. When we give to a person in need, it is the same as giving an offering to God.

When we harm others or fail to care for those in need, we are not showing our love for Christ. Let us serve the Lord by being generous in our service for Him. ~~

Thought for the Day

Lasting greatness is measured by God's standards.

For in this hope we were saved. But hope that is seen is no hope at all. Who hopes for what he already has? But if we hope for what we do not yet have, we wait for it patiently. *Romans 8:24-25 NIV*

~~ We were saved by hope, the glorious appearing of the great God and our Savior Jesus Christ. The believer has hope because he knows that all the pain and suffering of this world will one day be over.

We wait patiently for Christ to return as He promised. ~~

Thought for the Day

For the believer the best is to come.

Blessed are all those who put their trust in Him.
Psalm 2:12b NKJV

~~ We are blessed who put our trust in the Son of God. Christ is not only God's chosen King but He is our King. Let our hearts reflect our submissive love and devotion to our King. ~~

Thought for the Day

Blessed are those who trust in Christ.

For physical training is of some value, but godliness has value for all things, holding promise for both the present life and the life to come. *1 Timothy 4:8 NIV*

~~ Paul used an athletic illustration in his letter to Timothy. He explained that a Greek or Roman athlete had to train to win. Training for godliness involves spiritual exercise. If we put as much effort into our spiritual life as an athlete puts into his training, we will grow and accomplish much for the Lord.

Godliness has value for the present life and the life to come. ~~

Thought for the Day

Train every day for godliness.

He gives strength to the weary and increases the power of the weak. *Isaiah 40:29 NIV*

~~ With God anything is possible. He is the source of our every need. He knows how we feel and what we fear. God will provide the strength we need. If we trust ourselves, we will fail, but if we wait on the Lord by faith, we will receive strength for whatever difficulties we face. ~~

Thought for the Day

God is my strength.

"Fear not, for I am with you; be not dismayed, for I am your God. I will strengthen you, yes, I will help you, I will uphold you with my righteous right hand." *Isaiah 41:10 NKJV*

~~ As we read this scripture, we can sense God's love for His people and His desire to encourage them to trust Him for now and the future.

God has assured us that we are not to fear or become discouraged. He is our God and He strengthens us. He is our helper and our redeemer. God is our everything. ~~

Thought for the Day

God is the Alpha and Omega.

The fear of the Lord is the beginning of wisdom, and knowledge of the Holy One is understanding.
Proverbs 9:10 NIV

~~ We know that our Lord will give us knowledge and discernment when it comes to the decisions of life. To know the Holy One is to know His Word and to spend time with Him in prayer. When we respond to the Lord's wisdom, we will have a deeper knowledge and understanding of the Holy One. ~~

Thought for the Day

Wisdom comes from God.

"If you love me, you will obey what I command."
John 14:15 NIV

~~ Jesus is speaking to His disciples and preparing them for
the time He will not be with them in the flesh. If we love
the Lord, we will do as the Lord commanded His disciples,
we will obey His commands.

We are to pray in loving obedience, always honoring the
Lord's name. ~~

Thought for the Day

Love and honor the Lord.

The Lord is my strength and my song; he has become my salvation. He is my God, and I will praise Him, my father's God, and I will exalt Him.
Exodus 15:2 NIV

~~ This verse is part of a song that the Israelites sang when God saved them by parting the Red Sea allowing them to escape. Their enemies, the Egyptian army, drowned and with freedom certain, the children of Israel burst out in song and praise to the Lord. The people realized the Lord was their strength, their salvation and their God. They sang this hymn of praise to the Lord and about the Lord to exalt Him.

The victory over the Egyptians was a glorious victory, for it was the work of the Lord alone. We too can have glorious victory in our lives by trusting and obeying our Lord. ~~

Thought for the Day

God's victory is glorious.

"The LORD bless you and keep you; the LORD make His face shine upon you, and be gracious to you; the LORD lift up His countenance upon you, and give you peace." *Numbers 6:24-26 NKJV*

~~ We all need the blessings that the Lord gives to each of us. The Lord blesses and cares for us. He smiles upon us and gives us His grace. He hears us when we call on Him. Because of these blessings, we will receive peace in our hearts.

Those who share the Lord's truth to many or only one person at a time bless the world. ~~

Thought for the Day

May the Lord bless you.

Humble yourselves before the Lord, and He will lift you up.   *James 4:10 NIV*

~~ The Lord will lift us up, either in this life or the next life. "Humble yourselves, therefore, under God's mighty hand, that he may lift you up in due time." (*1 Peter 5:6 NIV*)

God will give us peace, when we humble ourselves before Him, confessing our sins and asking for forgiveness. In everything we do, let us humbly obey the Lord. ~~

Thought for the Day

Let us have humble hearts.

Our help is in the name of the Lord, the Maker of heaven and earth. *Psalm 124:8 NIV*

~~ Have you ever felt that your problems were over-whelming and there was no way out? There is always a way when you call upon the name of the Lord. He created the heaven and the earth and nothing is too hard for the Lord to resolve. ~~

Thought for the Day

The Lord never fails.

Cast your bread upon the waters, for after many days you will find it again. *Ecclesiastes 11:1 NIV*

~~ As believers in Christ, we live in faith and expect the unexpected. We cannot control circumstances. But we can trust God to be with us. Life is an adventure and has a certain amount of risk to it, and that is where our faith in God comes in.

We are given opportunities (casting our bread upon the waters) and we need to seize them. After many days we will find "our bread" again. Let us go forth with a spirit of trust and total faith in God. ~~

Thought for the Day

Trust and put your faith in God.

In the way of righteousness there is life; along that path is immortality.   *Proverbs 12:28 NIV*

~~ When we walk in the way of righteousness, our ethical conduct will conform to God's standard and moral character that comes from a right relationship to the Lord and His Word.

Our walk in the way of righteousness is the path to eternal life. ~~

Thought for the Day

Seek the path of righteousness.

Keep your lives free from the love of money and be content with what you have, because God has said, "Never will I leave you; never will I forsake you." *Hebrews 13:5 NIV*

~~ All the material things one can buy will never satisfy the heart. Only God can give us what we need. The love of money has caused terrific heartache and pain for many.

Strive to be content with what God has provided, and remember that money and possessions are only temporary.

God has given us the greatest of all gifts -- His promise that He will never leave us or forsake us. ~~

Thought for the Day

In God we are secure.

Trust in the Lord forever, for in Yah, the Lord, is everlasting strength.   *Isaiah 26:4 NKJV*

~~ Only in the Lord can we find strength to live our lives to God's glory here on earth. Put all your faith and trust in the Lord and you will find everlasting strength and salvation. ~~

Thought for the Day

In God is everlasting strength.

He has scattered abroad His gifts to the poor, His righteousness endures forever; His horn will be lifted high in honor. *Psalm 112:9 NIV*

~~ The man described in this Psalm was a righteous man. Because he was generous to the poor, the Lord allowed him to be admired by his peers.

All those faithful to God will be lifted high in honor. Their righteousness will endure forever. ~~

Thought for the Day

Honor God by helping those in need.

My soul weeps because of grief; Strengthen me according to your Word. *Psalm 119:28 NASB*

~~ This verse describes our feelings when we sin and disappoint God. When we sin, we are sinning against God.

Let us ask God to strengthen us so that we may do His will in our lives. ~~

Thought for the Day

Let us strive to please our Savior.

God Has Given Me a Song to Sing
Psalm 96:1 NIV

Words and music by Grace Knafel, Copyright, 1975

1. God has given me a song to sing of Jesus Christ the King
Let me tell you how He's with me every day.
He fills me from above with His peace and joy and love;
And I know, I know, I know He's here to stay.

Chorus: *(To be sung after every verse)*
He is the Shepherd, He is the Rock;
He is the Truth, the Life, the Way-ay-ay.
Great Things He hath done for us; Whereof we are glad!

2. Oh my friend out there do you have a care?
Let Jesus be your guide;
He's born it all; He knows it all, from Him you can't hide
"I love you" He will say, "Come unto me and pray;
And I'll show just how, just how to find the way."

3. Little children can't you see; He wants to sit you on His knee
And tell you all about His will for you.
He'll show you things to come and of the wonders He hath done;
And Christ the King will give will give you victory.

4. "It is finished," Jesus said, and then he bowed down His head,
"Father forgive them for they know not what they do.'
But in Your eternal plan it's full redemption for each man;
Oh crown Him Lord of Lords and King of Kings, won't you?

Thought for the Day

He is the truth, the life, the way.

If any of you lacks wisdom, he should ask God, who gives generously to all without finding fault, and it will be given to him.   *James 1:5 NIV*

~~ True wisdom comes from God. We cannot find it in self-help books or in anyone but God and His Word. This verse tells us that we are to seek wisdom from God, who gives generously to all without finding faults.

We pray and ask God to give us wisdom and understanding. When we are going through trials, wisdom helps us to understand how to use these circumstances for our good and God's glory. ~~

Thought for the Day

Ask and receive God's wisdom.

Command them to do good, to be rich in good
deeds, and to be generous and willing to share.
1 Timothy 6:18 NIV

~~ Having wealth comes with responsibility. We have the
same responsibly to share our material wealth, as did the
members of the Ephesian church. We are commanded to
use our wealth to do good to others. When we help those in
need, we enrich our lives spiritually. ~~

Thought for the Day

Everyone has something to share.

Two are better than one, because they have a good return for their work: If one falls down, his friend can help him up. But pity the man who falls and has no one to help him up! *Ecclesiastes 4:9-10 NIV*

~~ God designed companionship when He created Eve for Adam. God knew that man should not be alone.

Friendship is one of God's abundant blessings. A true friend will comfort you, encourage you and rejoice with you. Friends are given to us to help us live our lives. ~~

Thought for the Day

We need each other.

For I know whom I have believed and am persuaded that He is able to keep what I have committed to Him until that day. *2 Timothy 1:12b NKJV*

~~ Paul was in prison and facing death, but he knew God would use others to carry out the ministry. Paul knew that God was still in control. From prison, Paul continued to bear witness for the gospel of Jesus Christ. He had given his soul to Christ and Paul knew that Christ would keep what He had committed to him.

We are in difficult times; let us stand true to Christ and be willing to suffer for Him. ~~

Thought for the Day

Fully trust God.

The blessing of he LORD makes one rich, and He adds no sorrow with it.   *Proverbs 10:22 NKJV*

~~ Wealth is only a blessing when we use it according to God's will. With wealth come concerns and sorrow, but those who know that their blessings are from God do not have sorrow with it. ~~

Thought for the Day

Share your blessings.

Your Word is a lamp to my feet and a light to my path. *Psalm 119:105 NKJV*

~~ Studying and following God's Word will develop our faith. We walk by faith, knowing that God is with us and will never leave us. Obedience to God and His Word will keep us in the light while we are walking to our destination. ~~

Thought for the Day

God's Word is everlasting light.

"So then, don't be afraid. I will provide for you and your children." *Genesis 50:21a NIV*

~~ Now that their father was dead, the brothers feared that Joseph would retaliate against them for selling him into slavery. Joseph comforted his brothers and told them they had nothing to fear from him. He offered to provide not only for them but for their families.

Joseph, by forgiving his brothers, is an example of how God forgives and accepts us, whether we deserve it or not. ~~

Thought for the Day

Return good for evil.

For the kingdom of God is not a matter of talk but of power. *1 Corinthians 4:20 NIV*

~~ Paul was upset with the Corinthians because they talked a lot -- words were their religion. He was prepared to back up his talk with power and with deeds that would reveal their sins and God's holiness.

It is not what we say, but what we do with the power of God that rules in our hearts. Live so others will see the power of God working in you. ~~

Thought for the Day

Talk is powerless without deeds.

"Put your trust in the light while you have it."
John 12:36a NIV

~~ Jesus was speaking to His disciples. He knew that He would be leaving them soon. Jesus wanted them to put their trust in the light. In His light the disciples would know what was truth and could lead others to God.

Jesus Christ is the light of the world. It is only through Him that we find salvation. Be committed to Him in everything. Let your light be so bright that others will be able to see the path to God. ~~

Thought for the Day

Let your light shine.

Don't quit in hard times; pray all the harder. Help needy Christians; be inventive in hospitality.
Romans 12:13 The Message

~~ This text relays to us that we are not to overlook those that are in need. We are to show respect, we are to love, not only by communicating with them, but we are to help them. We honor God by doing what we have the capacity to do for others.

Even when we are not asked, we need to seek opportunities to practice hospitality. Let us always show kindness in welcoming guests or strangers into our homes. ~~

Thought for the Day

Honor God by helping others.

"Give, and it will be given to you. A good measure, pressed down, shaken together and running over, will be poured into your lap. For with the measure you use, it will be measured to you." *Luke 6:38 NIV*

~~ This verse is a reminder that we reap what we sow. If we live a life of giving, God will see to it that we receive. If we live a life only to get, we will lose. When our giving blesses others, we receive the greatest blessing of all.

If we treat others with love and respect, these qualities will return to us in good measure. ~~

Thought for the Day

Let us be a river of blessings to others.

"I am the resurrection and the life. He who believes in me will live, even though he dies."
John 11:25 NIV

~~ We will pass through the valley of the shadow of death,
but because Christ died on the cross for us, we will live. For
believers, death is not the end but a beginning of life forever
with God. This verse is confirmation that believers will one
day be raised from the dead. Believers in Christ have a
spiritual life death cannot conquer. ~~

Thought for the Day

Jesus has power over life and death.

Don't fret or worry. Instead of worrying, pray. Let petitions and praises shape your worries into prayers, letting God know your concerns.
Philippians 4:6 The Message

~~ When we find ourselves worrying about something, we need to approach God in prayer and worship. Our God is great and majestic and can solve any problem. Give your concerns to God and trust Him to take care of them. ~~

Thought for the Day

Turn worry into prayer.

To them God has chosen to make known among
the Gentiles the glorious riches of this mystery,
which is Christ in you, the hope of glory.
Colossians 1:27 NIV

~~ Jesus Christ came to earth, was rejected by people, and
was crucified. The fact that Jesus was resurrected from the
dead gives believers great assurance that death is not to be
feared. Believers will live with God.

Paul called God's plan a mystery because it was hidden until
Christ came. Christ is not hidden from you. Go to Him.
Don't delay, you do not want to miss being a part of God's
glorious kingdom. ~~

Thought for the Day

Christ is our hope of glory.

I want men everywhere to lift up holy hands in prayer, without anger or disputing. *1 Timothy 2:8 NIV*

~~ We can only have "holy hands" when we live a holy life. The Jewish men would extend their arms and their hands open toward heaven when they prayed.

Our prayers are to be without anger or disputing. We are to be forgiving of others like our Father in heaven who is forgiving of our sins. ~~

Thought for the Day

We can disagree without being disagreeable.

If we endure, we will also reign with Him. If we disown Him, He will also disown us. *2 Timothy 2:12 NIV*

~~ It is faith in Jesus Christ that sustains us as we endure suffering. Enduring leads to reigning in Glory with the Lord. Whatever suffering you are facing, don't turn away from God. We are promised a future with God where there is no death or heartache.

If we disown our Lord here, He will disown us before the Father. ~~

Thought for the Day

Endure and remain faithful.

"He has risen! He is not here." *Mark 16:6b NIV*

~~ When Mary Magdalene, Mary, the mother of James, and Salome arrived at the tomb, they were frightened to see that the stone had been rolled away. As they entered the tomb, a young man was there. He told them to not be afraid. Jesus the Nazarene was not there because He had risen.

Christ has risen, the tomb is empty, and the resurrection is a reality that Jesus Christ is everything He claimed to be. His resurrection conquered death. ~~

Thought for the Day

The tomb is empty.

"And I myself will be a wall of fire around it,"
declares the Lord, "and I will be its glory within."
Zechariah 2:5 NIV

~~ In *Zechariah 2:1-4* we read that Zechariah had a vision
that he saw a man measuring the city of Jerusalem. He was
told that Jerusalem would be a city without walls because of
the many men and livestock in it. The Lord has promised to
be a wall of fire around the city to protect His people.

Jerusalem will be restored in God's future kingdom. ~~

Thought for the Day

The Lord is glory now and forever.

"I am the gate; whoever enters through me will be saved." *John 10:9 NIV*

~~ We must come in by Jesus Christ, "the gate" and we will be saved. Salvation cannot be earned, bought, bribed, or gotten any other way except through Jesus Christ.

Jesus Christ not only gave His life for us, but He gives His life to us right now. He watches over us as a shepherd watches over his flock. We are able to enjoy abundant life in the pastures of the Lord. ~~

Thought for the Day

The Bible reveals the way of salvation.

"Now that you know these things, you will be blessed if you do them." *John 13:17 NIV*

~~ Jesus taught His disciples to serve. It is not enough to know this truth; we must practice serving others.

The only way to lasting happiness is to do what Jesus told us to do. We will receive true spiritual joy when we submit to the Lord, live a godly life and serve others. ~~

Thought for the Day

Do in this order: humbleness, holiness, and happiness.

I will say of the Lord, "He is my refuge and my fortress, my God, in whom I trust." *Psalm 91:2 NIV*

~~ The writer of this verse had faith in God to protect him through the dangers and obstacles of life. Is your faith strong enough to trust in the Lord to be your refuge and your fortress?

The Lord is our only deliverer, trust Him and let Him be your refuge and your fortress. ~~

Thought for the Day

Fear not, trust the Lord.

In fact, everyone who wants to live a godly life in Jesus Christ will be persecuted. *2 Timothy 3:12 NIV*

~~ In every city that Paul visited, he was persecuted because he was living a godly life. Paul was relaying to Timothy that people who obey and live for Christ would be persecuted.

Don't be discouraged if people criticize or hurt you because of what you believe and how you live your life. Pray for them and continue to love and honor God in everything. ~~

Thought for the Day

God is the only one we need to please.

You rule over the surging sea; when its waves
mount up, You still them.   *Psalm 89:9 NIV*

~~ God is there to still all our fears and give us His peace
even when we are struggling with all the perplexities of life.
All we have to do is to trust and obey Him. Even the mighty
waves of the sea obey and praise Him.

If our hearts belong to God, we can experience His perfect
peace that is beyond our understanding. ~~

Thought for the Day

Only from God comes perfect peace.

When Christ, who is your life, appears, then you will appear with Him in glory. *Colossians 3:4 NIV*

~~ Christ will return for His people. Those who belong to Christ have a responsibility to be prepared for His coming. They are to set their minds on things above, not on earthly things.

When Christ returns, His people will enter into eternal glory with Him. When He is revealed in His glory, they shall also be revealed in glory. ~~

Thought for the Day

Be ready to join Christ in glory.

Pleasant words are a honeycomb, sweet to the soul and healing to the bones.   *Proverbs 16:24 NIV*

~~ When gentle, kind words are spoken; it calms the mind and soul. Reckless words can stir up dissension and a gossip's words can cause division. Let us guard our words. They have the power to heal or do great damage.

In the Word of God we can find the cure for diseases that weaken our souls. ~~

Thought for the Day

Let your words be kind.

God picked you out as His from the very start.
2 Thessalonians 2:13b The Message

~~ It is not love alone that saves us. God loves the whole world, but the whole world is not saved. Love is revealed in grace and mercy. God in His grace gives us through Christ what we do not deserve. God in His mercy gave to Christ what we do deserve.

In this scripture Paul is encouraging the Thessalonian believers to remember that they were chosen by God from the very beginning. ~~

Thought for the Day

We are God's chosen.

I remembered my songs in the night. My heart mused and my spirit inquired. *Psalm 77:6 NIV*

~~ The writer of this scripture is comparing his present sadness to his former joys. He feared that God had rejected him. God sends out His message of love, but we have to be on the right wave length. We must be willing to receive His message and to obey it.

When doubts and fears dominate our thinking, our faith is lacking. We strengthen our faith by turning to God and studying His Word. ~~

Thought for the Day

Through prayer our focus turns to God.

God has poured out his love into our hearts by the Holy Spirit, whom he has given us. *Romans 5:5b NIV*

~~ The moment we receive Jesus Christ as our Savior, the Holy Spirit comes to dwell in our hearts. It is through the Holy Spirit that we experience God's amazing love.

As believers, we must grow in wisdom and knowledge of the Word of God. We grow by reading and obeying God's Word, the Holy Bible. ~~

Thought for the Day

Submit to the Holy Spirit.

Give me understanding, that I may observe Your law and keep it with all my heart. *Psalm 119:34 NASB*

~~ In order to receive understanding, we must get to know God better and discern His desires. We must pray for spiritual enlightenment so we may understand God's Word and God's will for our lives. ~~

Thought for the Day

Let our understanding lead to obedience.

In Love With My Savior
2 Peter 3:18 NIV

Words and music by Grace Knafel, Copyright, 2005

Chorus (to be sung at the beginning and after each verse)
I'm so in love, so deeply in love
With my Savior
Oh, I'm so in love, so deeply in love
With my Savior.

1. He shed his blood for me, so I can be forgiven
He died upon the tree, so I can go to heaven
He's coming back for me, in the good book it is written
Oh, I'm so in love with Him.

2. A wedding there will be, this bride is getting ready
My dress is made of silk,
He's washed and cleaned and groomed me
My lamp is filled with oil; there's no spot or wrinkle on me
Oh, I'm so in love with Him.

3. He supplies all my needs, according to His treasure
God's Word is now fulfilled; it is His Father's pleasure
He fills my heart with joy, complete beyond all measure
Oh, I'm so in love with Him.

Thought for the Day

Love Him.

"By this all men will know that you are my disciples, if you love one another." *John 13:35 NIV*

~~ People will know when we are walking with the Lord. It is love that is the true evidence that we belong to Jesus Christ. We follow His example by doing what He did.

Let our hearts be filled with love for others. Abraham Lincoln once said, "I feel sorry for the man who can't feel the whip when it is laid on the other man's back." ~~

Thought for the Day

Walk with man and God in love.

"So if the Son sets you free, you will be free indeed." *John 8:36 NIV*

~~ It is only through the power of His word that sinners can be set free. Jesus, Himself, is the truth that sets us free. His perfect truth frees us to be all that God meant us to be. ~~

Thought for the Day

Freedom is in Christ.

"Be perfect, therefore, as your heavenly Father is perfect." *Matthew 5:48 NIV*

~~ In this scripture the word *perfect* does not mean we can be sinlessly perfect, for that is impossible in this life. We can strive to be complete and mature, as we serve our heavenly Father. ~~

Thought for the Day

Divine characteristics come from God.

Lift your eyes and look to the heavens: Who created all these? *Isaiah 40:26a NIV*

~~ When we realize the greatness of God, we will be able to see everything else in life in its proper perspective. There is nothing equal or greater than our God.

"Early this morning I watched that gorgeous red-orange ball come up over the ocean as the bright-white full moon was setting in the west. The sea gulls and pelicans were dancing in the air, and the gentle tropical breeze provided a coolant as it touched my face. All this was yet another affirmation of the recognizable signs of God's marvelous creativity and His love. Praise be to Him." *D. Mitchell* ~~

Thought for the Day

God created the heavens and the earth.

So then, the law is holy, and the commandment is holy, righteous and good. *Romans 7:12 NIV*

~~ We know there is sin. Do we realize the sinfulness of sin? We excuse our sins with words like "mistakes" or "weaknesses." Substituting different words does not change the severity of sin.

We must realize that we have to oppose sin in order to live in victory. ~~

Thought for the Day

The law shows the sinfulness of sin.

How long will you waver between two opinions? If the Lord is God, follow Him. *1 Kings 18:21b NIV*

~~ In this Scripture Elijah's purpose was not only to expose the false god Baal but also to bring the people back to the Lord.

Elijah prepared a sacrifice for God and prayed to God to send fire to burn the sacrifice. God sent fire and the sacrifice burned. Worshipers of Baal prepared a sacrifice. They prayed to Baal to send fire, but the fire never came.

When the people saw that God had sent the fire, they acknowledged that He was the true God. ~~

Thought for the Day

God is true now and forever.

"When his offering is a sacrifice of a peace offering
...... he shall offer it without blemish before the
Lord." *Leviticus 3:1 NKJV*

~~ A person would represent a peace offering, to establish
fellowship between himself and the Lord. Our peace
offering is surrendering ourselves to the Lord, holding
nothing back ~~

Thought for the Day

Let us be holy and pleasing to God.

The Lord lives! Blessed be my Rock! Let God be exalted, the Rock of my salvation! *2 Samuel 22:47 NKJV*

~~ In this verse David is praising the Lord by declaring that the Lord is alive. He was witnessing to the people that their dead idols, the work of man's hands, could not save them or protect them.

There is only one rock of salvation, the living God. God is alive. He thinks about us and He cares for us and He should always be first in our lives. ~~

Thought for the Day

God is the true rock of salvation.

Many of the Samaritans from that town believed in Him because of the woman's testimony, "He told me everything I ever did." *John 4:39 NIV*

~~ Jesus spoke to the woman when she came to draw water from the well. He told her everything she had ever done. She told other Samaritans about Jesus and many believed her. Despite the woman's reputation, many went to hear Jesus speak and they too believed in Him.

The woman's life was changed forever after she met Jesus, just as our lives will change forever when we accept Jesus Christ as our Lord and Savior. ~~

Thought for the Day

Testimony can lead others to Christ.

Since we have now been justified by His blood, how much more shall we be saved from God's wrath through Him! *Romans 5:9 NIV*

~~ Because of Jesus Christ, we are freed from God's wrath in this life and the life to come. A saved person has been cleansed by the blood of Christ. ~~

Thought for the Day

Saved by the blood of Christ.

For we know that since Christ was raised from the dead, he cannot die again; death no longer has mastery over Him. *Romans 6:9 NIV*

~~ Christ paid the penalty for sin, and broke the power of sin. Sin and death have no power over Christ. Because Christ died for us, sin and death have no power over us. ~~

Thought for the Day

Christ conquered sin and death.

"In the same way, any of you who does not give up everything he has cannot be my disciple."
Luke 14:33 NIV

~~ A disciple of Christ is devoted to Him. Jesus said that the one who keeps God's commandments is one who loves God. Because a disciple loves God, he puts God first in his life. He does not let obstacles get in the way of his service to Christ. ~~

Thought for the Day

Is God first?

For everything that was written in the past was written to teach us, so that through endurance and the encouragement of the Scriptures we might have hope.   *Romans 15:4 NIV*

~~ God's Word gives us guidance for the present and the future. The more we learn about what God did in the past, the more trust we will have about the future. In His Word we find encouragement and hope. ~~

Thought for the Day

God is our hope.

If we confess our sins, He is faithful and just and will forgive us our sins and purify us from all unrighteousness.   *1 John 1:9 NIV*

~~ God is just and faithful to His promise to forgive our sins and purify us from all unrighteousness. When we sin, we are sinning against God. If our confession is sincere, God cleanses our heart by His Spirit and through His Word. ~~

Thought for the Day

Confess and forsake sin.

"I tell you the truth, whoever hears my Word and believes Him who sent me has eternal life and will not be condemned; he has crossed over from death to life." *John 5:24 NIV*

~~ To hear God's Word and believe means salvation; to reject His Word means condemnation. Believers will have eternal life; they will never die spiritually nor come into judgment~~

Thought for the Day

Hear His Word and believe.

"Can any of you prove me guilty of sin? If I am telling the truth, why don't you believe me?"
John 8:46 NIV

~~ The Pharisees did not believe Jesus because they did not belong to God. They belonged to Satan and there is no truth in him. Because Jesus told the truth, they did not believe Him. ~~

Thought for the Day

God is flawless.

"For he who touches you, touches the apple of His eye." *Zechariah 2:8b NASB*

~~ Believers are very precious to God. If we treat other believers unkindly, we are also treating God the same way. Any good that we do for others, we also do for God. ~~

Thought for the Day

Guard your actions.

Listen to my prayer, O God, do not ignore my plea; hear me and answer me. My thoughts trouble me and I am distraught. *Psalm 55:1-2 NIV*

~~ David had sinned and separated himself from God. He was pleading for God to hear and answer his prayers. He was asking God, his Savior, to not reject or forsake him.

God will never reject our prayers or withhold His amazing love from us. ~~

Thought for the Day

Praise be to God.

"Then you will know the truth, and the truth will set you free." *John 8:32 NIV*

~~ The only way to find the truth is to study God's Word. When we obey His Word, we grow in spiritual knowledge. Jesus himself is the truth that sets us free. It is through Jesus that we find the way to eternal life with God. If we do not know the truth, we are an easy prey for deception. ~~

Thought for the Day

Jesus sets us free.

Being confident of this, that He who began a good work in you will carry it on to completion until the day of Christ Jesus. *Philippians 1:6 NIV*

~~ The God who began a good work in us continues it throughout our lifetime. It will be finished when we meet Him face to face. God's work for us began when Christ died on the cross in our place. His work in us began when we accepted Jesus Christ as our Savior. The Holy Spirit lives in us, making our lives more like Christ every day. ~~

Thought for the Day

God never gives up on us.

Moses answered the people, "Do not be afraid. Stand firm and you will see the deliverance the Lord will bring you today." *Exodus 14:13 NIV*

~~ Moses was a man of great faith and he knew Pharaoh's army was no threat to God. He told the people to not be afraid and to stand firm and the Lord would deliver them. God divided the Red Sea and His people walked to safety, but Pharaoh's army was destroyed.

There is nothing in our lives that God cannot deliver us from. Don't be afraid, stand firm and you will see the deliverance God has promised. ~~

Thought for the Day

Faith obeys and brings glory to God.

"Even to your old age and gray hairs I am He, I am He who will sustain you. I have made you and I will carry you; I will sustain you and I will rescue you." *Isaiah 46:4 NIV*

~~ What a wonderful promise we are given in this scripture. God is promising us that from the time we are born He is there to sustain us and carry us. His love for each of us is so enduring that He will care for us even through death. ~~

Thought for the Day

God is always present.

When anxiety was great within me, Your
consolation brought joy to my soul. *Psalm 94:19 NIV*

~~ The Lord is our refuge and strength. We turn to the
Lord to not escape being responsible, but to pray for
strength to overcome fear and anxiety. Only God can bring
true peace and joy into our hearts. ~~

Thought for the Day

God is peace and joy.

Preach the word; be prepared in season and out of season; correct, rebuke and encourage -- with great patience and careful instruction. *2 Timothy 4:2 NIV*

~~ Paul told Timothy to preach the gospel so it would spread throughout the world. We need to be ready to serve God, any time or any place. As believers we are to spread the gospel to those who do not know Christ. Christ will return and His believers need to be ready to meet Him. ~~

Thought for the Day

Are you ready?

"Freely you have received, freely give."
Matthew 10:8b NIV

~~ God has freely given us everything we have, including life. We are to give freely to others of our time, love and possessions. When we give back a portion of what we have been given, we are expressing our love and devotion to God and our fellowman. ~~

Thought for the Day

Share your blessings.

Your attitude should be the same as that of Christ
Jesus. *Philippians 2:5 NIV*

~~ An unknown man once said, "Give your mind to Christ
that you may be guided by His wisdom." If we have the
same attitude as Christ, we will be humble and willing to
serve others. Christ humbled himself and died on the cross
for our salvation. ~~

Thought for the Day

Are you like-minded with Christ?

"Take my yoke upon you and learn from me, for I am gentle and humble in heart, and you will find rest for your souls." *Matthew 11:29 NIV*

~~ When we take God's yoke upon us and we learn from Him, we will be given rest. The rest that is promised to us is love, healing and peace with God. As we learn more about God from studying His Word, we find a deeper peace with Him. ~~

Thought for the Day

Trust your soul to God.

We do not know what we ought to pray for, but the Spirit Himself intercedes for us with groans that words cannot express. *Romans 8:26b NIV*

~~ When we pray we receive help from the Spirit of God. Because we do not know what we should pray for, the Spirit intercedes for us. ~~

Thought for the Day

The Holy Spirit guides us to God.

Our help is in the name of the Lord, who made heaven and earth. *Psalm 124:8 NASB*

~~ The death and resurrection of Jesus Christ ended the reign of sin and death. His resurrection has allowed us to walk in freedom. ~~

Thought for the Day

Our help is from our Creator.

When Jesus Found Me
Revelation 3:5 NIV

Words and music by Lewis C. Briggs, Copyright 1986

1. The angels up in glory
Rejoiced when Jesus found me
In the book of life my name is written there
He snatched me from the burnings
Is grooming me for heaven
Eternity with Jesus I shall share.

Refrain
Oh, I know that Jesus loves me
He tells me in His Word
His life giving Spirit floods my soul
He has marked the path before me
And with His Word He'll guide me
To my new home beyond the other shore.

2. Just heed the Holy Scriptures
It is a great blessing
To eat and drink at the table of the Lord
His way is ever righteous
With those who walk before Him
His path is filled with treasurers evermore.

Lewis C. Briggs loved the Lord and was the father of Donna Mitchell and Gracie Knafel. We are honored to have a copy of his composition included in this book He was 79 when God gave him this song and he lived to be 96 years old. You can also listen to its melody at→ www.gracesongs.net.

Thought for the Day

We are safe with Jesus.

The end of all things is near. Therefore be clear-minded and self-controlled so that you can pray.
1 Peter 4:7 NIV

~~ Franklin Graham wrote: "Prayer is the most important action any of us can take for the cause of Christ in this world." Our nation is in great spiritual danger. We must call on God to heal this country, forgive our sins and be prepared for the coming of Christ.

Time is running out. Don't wait to pray. ~~

Thought for the Day

Seek the Lord in prayer.

Discretion will protect you, and understanding will guard you. *Proverbs 2:11 NIV*

~~ We are capable of destroying ourselves because of our lack of discretion. The more knowledge we have from God's Word the better our discretion will be. Discretion gives us the freedom to decide what should be done in a particular situation. God-centered discretion is our protection from making wrong decisions. Understanding His Word guards us from making wrong decisions. ~~

Thought for the Day

Is your discretion God-centered?

Let us then approach the throne of grace with
confidence, so that we may receive mercy and find
grace to help us in our time of need.
Hebrews 4:16 NIV

~~ The apostle Paul shows us the privileges of the New
Testament above those of the Old Testament. In the Old
Testament only the high priest was allowed to approach
God. The New Testament allows us to approach God with
confidence and without fear.

God's mercy is ours for the taking because Christ died for
our sins. God's grace is given to us after we have received
His mercy. We are to call on God for mercy and grace when
needed. ~~

Thought for the Day

Pray with bold assurance.

Whatever you do, work at it with all your heart, as working for the Lord, not for men. *Colossians 3:23 NIV*

~~ God will reward us for doing honorable and faithful work. We will receive an inheritance of eternal life for faithfully serving Christ. Let us approach work as a servant of Christ.

Whatever work God has given us, we are to work at it with all our hearts. Let us remember we are not working for men, but for God. ~~

Thought for the Day

Our inheritance comes from God, not man.

But we have this treasure in earthen vessels, so that the surpassing greatness of the power will be of God and not from ourselves. *2 Corinthians 4:7 NASB*

~~ God's shining light illuminates our hearts. Our bodies are frail and easily broken like fragile clay jars. Only God has the power to mend our souls. The great treasure we have is the light and salvation of God.

We are to be continually dependent on God. We have nothing but what we receive from Him. Any good that we do comes from the power of God, not from ourselves. ~~

Thought for the Day

All glory belongs to God.

If we say that we have no sin, we are deceiving ourselves and the truth is not in us. If we confess our sins, He is faithful and righteous to forgive our sins and to cleanse us from all unrighteousness.
John 1:8-9 NASB

~~ John is speaking to the false teachers who were walking in sin. They were teaching the people that they did not have a sinful nature; therefore, they could not sin. To say we are without sin is to deceive ourselves and to deny the truth. Jesus Christ is the truth. It is only through Him that we can confess our sins and He will cleanse and forgive us. ~~

Thought for the Day

God is faithful and forgiving.

Let the wicked forsake his way and the unrighteous man his thoughts; and let him return to the Lord, and He will have compassion on him, and to our God, for He will abundantly pardon. *Isaiah 55:7 NASB*

~~ Forsaking sin is an integral part of seeking the Lord. "Wash yourselves, make yourselves clean; remove the evil of your deeds from my sight." (*Isaiah 1:16 NASB*) When we go before the Lord and acknowledge that we have sinned, He shows us grace and mercy. The Lord is compassionate and forgiving to those who seek Him. ~~

Thought for the Day

Only God can pardon.

I love God because he listened to me, listened as I begged for mercy. *Psalm 116:1 The Message*

~~ The author of this scripture is thanking God for hearing his prayer. God listens to our prayers and He answers. Our love for God grows as we experience His answers to our prayers. ~~

Thought for the Day

Shout praise to the Lord.

For out of the overflow of the heart the mouth speaks. *Matthew 12:34b NIV*

~~ When we fill our hearts with God's love, it will be apparent to others when we speak. It is also apparent to others, if our hearts are not filled with God's love. Are you aware of what is in your heart? Only the Holy Spirit can cleanse our hearts.

"The good man out of the good treasure of his heart brings forth what is good; and the evil man out of the evil treasure brings forth what is evil; for his mouth speaks from that which fills his heart." (*Luke 6:45 NASB*) ~~

Thought for the Day

Fill your heart with good treasure.

My people are destroyed for lack of knowledge.
Hosea 4:6 NASB

~~ The religious leaders were engaged in wrongdoing and were teaching the people false doctrine. The people were facing destruction because they did not know the difference between false doctrine and true doctrine.

Do not let yourself be a victim of sinful leaders. Search the Word of God and you will know what is true and what is false. ~~

Thought for the Day

Seek knowledge in God's Word.

Do not withhold good from those who deserve it, when it is in your power to act. *Proverbs 3:27 NIV*

~~ This verse reminds me of the story of the Good Samaritan that aided a traveler who had been beaten and robbed. A priest and a Levite also saw the traveler but they crossed over to the other side of the road. The Samaritan did not withhold good from the injured man. He cared for the man's wounds and paid the innkeeper to care for him until he returned.

We are not to withhold good when it is in our power to do so. ~~

Thought for the Day

Let us show mercy to those in need.

The mind of the intelligent seeks knowledge, but the mouth of fools feeds on folly. *Proverbs 15:14 NASB*

~~Those that love the Lord seek His knowledge by reading and studying God's Word. "The mind of the prudent acquires knowledge, and the ear of the wise seeks knowledge." (*Proverbs 18:15, NASB*)

All of us are exposed to some foolish people. We know them by their actions. Foolish people feed on the things of the world instead of the things of God. ~~

Thought for the Day

God is knowledge.

The Lord does not look at the things man looks at. Man looks at the outward appearance, but the Lord looks at the heart. *1 Samuel 16:7b NIV*

~~ The Lord sent Samuel to Jesse of Bethlehem to anoint one of his sons as king. The Lord had rejected Saul as king over Israel. Jesse had seven of his sons pass before Samuel, but none were chosen by the Lord to be king. Samuel asked if there were any more sons. They sent for the youngest son, David, who was tending the sheep. The outward appearance of David was not important to God. God looked into David's heart and anointed him as king of Israel.

Only God can see what is in the heart and only He can accurately judge people. ~~

Thought for the Day

Is your heart pleasing to God?

INDEX

102 - Jeremiah 17:7 NIV
102 - Jeremiah 17:8 NIV
101 - Jeremiah 29:13 NIV
120 - Jeremiah 31:3 NASB
049 - Job 22:23 The Message
225 - 1 John 1:9 NIV
086 - 1 John 2:17 NASB
161 - 1 John 4:16 NIV
009 - 1 John 4:19 NIV
148 - 1 John 5:14-15 NIV
247 - John 1:8-9 NASB
220 - John 4:39 NIV
226 - John 5:24 NIV
042 - John 7:17 NKJV
230 - John 8:32 NIV
213 - John 8:36 NIV
227 - John 8:46 NIV
200 - John 10:9 NIV
193 - John 11:25 NIV
190 - John 12:36a NIV
201 - John 13:17 NIV
212 - John 13:35 NIV
134 - John 14:2 NIV
100 - John 14:6-7 The Message
170 - John 14:15 NIV
015 - John 14:27 NASB
038 - John 15:4-5 NASB
079 - John 15:13-14 The Message
017 - John 16:23 NIV
020 - John 16:26-27 NIV
083 - John 16:33b The Message
124 - Joshua 3:4a NIV
217 - 1 Kings 18:21b NIV
105 - Lamentations 3:22 NIV
218 - Leviticus 3:1 NKJV
145 - Luke 1:37 NKJV
192 - Luke 6:38 NIV
250 - Luke 6:45 NASB
036 - Luke 11:28 The Message
223 - Luke 14:33 NIV
113 - Luke 21:28 NIV
094 - Mark 3:35 NIV
109 - Mark 7:5 The Message

109 - Mark 7:6-8 The Message
156 - Mark 8:34-35 NIV
163 - Mark 9:41 NKJV
198 - Mark 16:6b NIV
097 - Matthew 1:21 NIV
041 - Matthew 5:3 NASB
076 - Matthew 5:20 The Message
126 - Matthew 5:41 NIV
214 - Matthew 5:48 NIV
149 - Matthew 6:9a NIV
099 - Matthew 6:24 The Message
001 - Matthew 7:7 NASB
056 - Matthew 7:12 The Message
236 - Matthew 10:8b NIV
014 - Matthew 11:28 NASB
238 - Matthew 11:29 NIV
250 - Matthew 12:34b NIV
048 - Matthew 16:26-27 NASB
160 - Matthew 18:20 The Message
132 - Nehemiah 8:10 NIV
172 - Numbers 6:24-26 NKJV
089 - Numbers 23:19 NIV
040 - 1 Peter 3:4 The Message
129 - 1 Peter 3:9 NIV
242 - 1 Peter 4:7 NIV
107 - 1 Peter 4:12-14 The Message
080 - 1 Peter 5:5 NIV
173 - 1 Peter 5:6 NIV
211 - 2 Peter 3:18 NIV
003 - Philippians 1:4-5 NIV
231 - Philippians 1:6 NIV
082 - Philippians 1:7 NASB
092 - Philippians 2:3-4 NIV
237 - Philippians 2:5 NIV
005 - Philippians 3:13 NKJV
143 - Philippians 3:15-16 The Message
194 - Philippians 4:6 The Message
034 - Philippians 4:8 NASB
045 - Philippians 4:11-12 The Message
046 - Philippians 4:19 NIV
117 - Proverbs 1:33 NIV
243 - Proverbs 2:11 NIV
110 - Proverbs 3:5-6 The Message

258

About the author

Hatha Lee Brown was born and raised in South Florida and moved to Wisconsin in 2008. She and her husband, Terry Brown, are both active in their church and community service. They have blended their two families; and, together, they have four wonderful children, seven lovely grandchildren and five beloved pets.

Hatha endured the deaths of a teenage daughter, a sister and a husband. She also survived the devastation of two hurricanes that ruined her Florida home in 2004. She overcame these adversities through her faith in God, the support of her church, her family and her friends. She combined her love for the Lord with her writing talents to bring about this composition. Her heart is with the prison ministries; and she plans to plant her work in penitentiaries with the hope of leading souls to Christ.

She has written several articles. <u>To God Be The Glory</u> is her first published devotional.

LaVergne, TN USA
09 March 2011

219335LV00003B/1/P